CONTEMPORARY MORAL PROBLEMS

War, Terrorism, and Torture

THIRD EDITION

CONTEMPORARY MORAL PROBLEMS

War, Terrorism, and Torture

JAMES E. WHITE
St. Cloud State University

THOMSON
WADSWORTH

AUSTRALIA • BRAZIL • CANADA • MEXICO • SINGAPORE
SPAIN • UNITED KINGDOM • UNITED STATES

THOMSON

—✦—

WADSWORTH

Contemporary Moral Problems: War, Terrorism, and Torture, **Third Edition**
James E. White

Philosophy Editor: *Worth Hawes*
Development Editor: *Ian Lague*
Assistant Editor: *Patrick Stockstill*
Editorial Assistant: *Kamilah Lee*
Technology Project Manager: *Julie Aguilar*
Marketing Manager: *Christina Shea*
Marketing Assistant: *Mary Anne Payumo*
Marketing Communications Manager:
    Darlene Amidon-Brent
Project Manager, Editorial Production:
    Matt Ballantyne

Creative Director: *Rob Hugel*
Art Director: *Maria Epes*
Print Buyer: *Linda Hsu*
Permissions Editor: *Mardell Glinski-Schultz*
Production Service: *Aaron Downey,*
    Matrix Productions Inc.
Copy Editor: *Ivan Weiss*
Cover Designer: *Yvo*
Compositor: *International Typesetting*
    and Composition

Library of Congress Control Number: 2007940276

ISBN-13: 978-0-495-55322-9
ISBN-10: 0-495-55322-0

For more information about our products,
contact us at:
Thomson Learning Academic Resource Center
1-800-423-0563
For permission to use material from this text or
product, submit a request online at
http://www.thomsonrights.com.
Any additional questions about permissions
can be submitted by e-mail to
thomsonrights@thomson.com.

CONTENTS

CONTEMPORARY MORAL PROBLEMS
War, Terrorism, and Torture

War and Terrorism

- **Introduction**

INTRODUCTION

Factual Background

The history of humans is a sad chronicle of war and terrorism. Almost every year there has been a war or an act of terrorism somewhere in the world. Thus far, there have been no nuclear or biological wars, but the weapons are there ready to use. India and Pakistan have been fighting over a disputed area of Kashmir for over fifty years and continue to do so. Israel has fought several wars and continues to fight the Palestinians on a daily basis. The Palestinians respond with suicide bombers. There was a war in Bosnia generated by ethnic differences. Saddam Hussein invaded Kuwait and the result was the Gulf War. A short list of the major wars in the twentieth century includes World Wars I and II, the Korean War, the Vietnam War, and a bitter struggle in Afghanistan when Russian forces tried to invade. Iran and Iraq fought a bloody war, with Iraq being armed and supported by the United States.

Constant war continues in the twenty-first century. In 2001, U.S. and British forces invaded Afghanistan to capture Osama bin Laden and remove the Taliban regime, which had supported the al Qaeda terrorist organization responsible for the 9/11 attacks. After six years of fighting, U.S. troops were still looking for bin Laden and battling Taliban insurgents who remained in mountain strongholds. In 2003, U.S., British, and other troops invaded and occupied Iraq, claiming that Iraq had weapons of mass destruction and ties to al Qaeda. After four years of occupation by the U.S. and British forces, the Iraq War had turned into a civil war with no end in sight. (See the Problem Case.) In 2006, Israel fought a short war in Lebanon that killed over a thousand people, damaged Lebanese infrastructure, and displaced more than 900,000 Lebanese.

Terrorist attacks have dramatically increased in the twenty-first century. Suicide bombings, missile strikes, shootings, and other attacks have become a frequent occurrence in Iraq and Israel. Sometimes soldiers or the police are killed, but many times it is civilians who die. In 2004, Israeli missiles killed Sheik Ahmed Yassin, the spiritual leader of the militant group Hamas, which Israel claimed was responsible for terrorist bombings in Israel. In 2004, ten bombs ripped through four commuter trains in Madrid during the morning rush hour, killing nearly 200 and wounding more than 1,400. This was the deadliest terrorist attack on a European target since World War II. On September 11, 2001, nineteen terrorists hijacked four airplanes. They crashed two of the planes into the World Trade Center in New York City, destroying the twin towers. It is estimated that 3,000 people were killed. A third plane hit the Pentagon, killing nearly 200 workers. The fourth plane crashed in rural southwest Pennsylvania after the passengers overpowered the terrorists. A total of 266 people were killed on the four planes. This was the most devastating terrorist attack in U.S. history. Some compared it to the Japanese attack on Pearl Harbor that resulted in war with Japan, a war that ended shortly after Hiroshima and Nagasaki were destroyed with nuclear bombs in August 1945.

The United States produced convincing evidence that Osama bin Laden and his al Qaeda network of terrorists were responsible for the 9/11 attacks. On September 23, 2001, bin Laden issued a statement urging his followers to remain steadfast on the path of jihad against the infidels, that is, the United States and her allies. In 2007, bin Laden had still not been captured, and he continued to issue videos declaring war against the infidels.

This was only the latest and most shocking of a series of terrorist attacks on U.S. citizens and servicemen. On October 12, 2000, a terrorist bombing killed seventeen U.S. sailors aboard the U.S.S. Cole as it refueled in Yemen's port of Aden. The United States said that bin Laden was the prime suspect. On August 7, 1998, there were car bombings of U.S. embassies in Nairobi, Kenya, and Dar es Salaam, Tanzania. More than 5,500 people were injured and 224 were killed. Once again the prime suspect was Osama bin Laden. In June, 1996, a truck bomb exploded outside the Khobar Towers in Dharan, Saudi Arabia, killing 19 U.S. servicemen and wounding hundreds of other people. Members of a radical Lebanese terrorist group, Hezbollah, were indicted for the attack. On February 26, 1993, a bomb exploded in a parking garage below the World Trade Center, killing 6 people and wounding more than 1,000. Six radical Muslim terrorists were convicted and sentenced to life in prison. On April 19, 1995, a federal building in Oklahoma City was destroyed by a truck bomb. There were 168 deaths. Timothy J. McVeigh was executed for the attack and Terry L. Nichols was sentenced to life in prison. On December 21, 1998, Pam Am flight 103 exploded over Lockerbie, Scotland, killing 270 people onboard. Two Libyan intelligence officers were accused of planting a suitcase containing the bomb. One was convicted in February 2001 and the other was set free.

THE READINGS

A traditional and important position on war and terrorism is pacifism. Pacifism can take different forms. Douglas P. Lackey distinguishes between four different types of pacifism: (1) the view that all killing is wrong, (2) the view that all violence is wrong, (3) the view that personal violence is always wrong, but political violence is sometimes morally right, and (4) the view that personal violence is sometimes morally permissible, but war is always morally wrong. Albert Schweitzer's position is an example of the first type of pacifism; he held that all killing is wrong because all life is sacred. Mohandas Gandhi's pacifism is an example of the second type because he opposed all violence. According to Lackey, a problem with both of these views is that sometimes killing or violence is required to save lives. For example, shouldn't a terrorist airplane hijacker be killed or restrained to prevent the hijacker from crashing the plane and killing all the passengers? The third view that condemns personal violence but allows political violence is attributed to St. Augustine. But this view has a problem with personal self-defense. Most people would agree that personal violence is justified in defense of one's life, as in the case of the terrorist airplane hijacker. The kind of pacifism that Lackey supports is the fourth view, which condemns all war as morally wrong but allows some personal violence. But this antiwar pacifism has a problem, too. Why can't some wars be justified by appealing to some great moral good such as political freedom? Certainly the Revolutionary War in America (to use Lackey's own example) is defended in this way.

Another important view on war is just war theory. Medieval Christian theologians called Scholastics originally formulated the theory, and it has been discussed ever since. The theory distinguishes between two questions about war. First, there is the question about the right to go to war, called *jus ad bellum,* or "right to war": What are the conditions that justify going to war? Second, there is the question about the right conduct in war, called *jus in bello,* or "right in war": How should combatants conduct themselves in fighting a war?

As William V. O'Brien explains it just war theory has two components, one concerned with the right to go to war and the other with the conduct of war. Three main conditions have to be met to establish the right to go to war: (1) the war must be declared by a competent authority, (2) there must be a just cause, and (3) there must be a right intention that ultimately aims at peace. The just cause condition is subdivided into four more conditions: the substance of the just cause, the form of the just cause, the proportionality of ends and means, and the requirement of the exhaustion of peaceful remedies. The substance of the just cause is the reason for going to war, such as "to protect the innocent from unjust attack." This reason could be given to justify going to war against Germany in World War II. The form of the just cause is either defensive or offensive. Defensive wars are easier to justify than offensive ones. O'Brien notes, however, that offensive wars of vindictive justice against infidels or heretics were once permitted. The requirement of proportionality has to do with general means and ends; basically the idea is that the ultimate end, such as political freedom or a democratic society, must be sufficiently good to justify the evil of warfare. The fourth requirement is that going to war should be a last resort after all peaceful remedies, such as negotiation, mediation, and arbitration, have failed.

Two basic principles limit conduct in a just war, the principle of proportion and the principle of discrimination. The principle of proportion says that the intermediate military ends, such as the capture of an enemy position, must justify the means used, such as the firing of rockets. The principle of discrimination prohibits intentional attacks on noncombatants and nonmilitary targets. This principle is the subject of much debate, as we will see.

Pacifism and just war theory have dominated discussions of war and terrorism in Western thought. Both of these positions developed in the tradition of Christianity. But there is another important doctrine about war that comes from Islam and is used to justify both war and terrorism. This is the Islamic doctrine of jihad. Although *jihad* is often translated as "holy war," this is not exactly what the term means. According to Michael G. Knapp (see the Suggested Readings), the jihad means struggle or striving in the path of God for a noble cause. The classic view of jihad allowed defensive war against the enemies of Islam, but it did not sanction the killing of all non-Muslims or even their conversion by force. Knapp quotes the Koran (2:256): "There is no compulsion in religion." Killing other Muslims could only be justified by classifying them as non-Muslims (e.g., as apostates or rebels). He notes that the Islamic law tradition was very hostile toward terrorism and severely punished rebels who attacked innocent victims.

Osama bin Laden (see the Suggested Readings) has tried to justify attacks on the United States by appealing to the doctrine of jihad, which allows attacking enemies of Islam. He says that he and his followers are attacking America "because you attacked us and continue to attack us." He gives a long list of places where the alleged attacks have occurred, including Palestine, Somalia, Chechnya, Lebanon, Iraq, and Afghanistan. He says that the Palestinians are fighting to regain the land taken away from them by Israel. American infidels are occupying holy places in Saudi Arabia—namely, the cities of Mecca and Medina—and fighting a war of annihilation against Iraq, which for 500 years was the heart of an Islamic empire. He goes on to morally condemn American society as a cesspool of usury, sexual debauchery, drug addiction, gambling, prostitution, and so on. He concludes by arguing that the United States violates human rights while claiming to uphold them.

Laurie Calhoun applies just war theory to terrorism, focusing on political and moral/religious terrorists. She does not argue that terrorism is morally wrong. Rather, she wants to show how just war theory can be used by terrorists to defend their actions, at least to themselves and their followers, using the very same theory that democratic nations use to justify their military campaigns, which kill innocent civilians. To see how they can do this, we need to look more closely at just war theory and particularly the doctrine of double effect. How can a nation justify dropping bombs on another nation when this act results in the killing of innocent civilians? If the principle of discrimination is understood as absolutely forbidding killing innocents, then no modern war could be justified. O'Brien and Lackey both make this point in the readings. To justify killing innocents, just war theorists appeal to the Catholic doctrine of double effect. (This doctrine has already been discussed in the Introduction to Chapter 3.) The doctrine distinguishes between two effects of an action: an intended effect and one that is foreseen but not intended (a side effect). The doctrine says that as long as the intended consequence of an act is good (e.g., winning a war or saving lives), then a bad foreseen consequence (e.g., the death of innocents) is morally allowed, provided this bad consequence is not intended. Calhoun argues that terrorists can use this sort of reasoning to justify their actions, as Timothy McVeigh did when he characterized the deaths of innocent people in the Oklahoma City bombing as "collateral damage." In other words, she argues, "just war" rationalizations are available to everyone—bin Laden as well as President Bush. Terrorists can present themselves to their followers as warriors for justice, and not as mere murderers or vigilantes.

Unlike Calhoun, Louise Richardson gives us a precise definition of terrorism. It simply means deliberately and violently targeting civilians for political purposes. The point of doing this is to send a political message to an audience that is not the same as the victims. To do this, the act and the victim usually have symbolic significance. To use her example, the Twin Towers and the Pentagon targeted in the 9/11 attacks were seen as icons of America's economic and military power, and this symbolism enhanced the shock value of the attacks. She denies that terrorists are irrational or insane. In fact, they attempt to justify their actions in various ways.

Claudia Card has no difficulty seeing the 9/11 attacks as terrorist and evil, but she doubts that the war on terrorism is the appropriate response. Terrorism is not an identifiable agent, and it is not clear what kinds of terrorism count as legitimate targets. For example, is a war on terrorism a justifiable response to domestic battering? If not, then similar objections may apply to the war on public terrorism. A more appropriate response, in her view, would be to hunt down those responsible for the planning and support of the attacks and bring them to trial by international tribunals.

David Luban discusses more problems with the war on terrorism. Luban agrees with Card that the current fight against terrorism does not fit the traditional model of a just war. Instead, the war on terrorism uses a new hybrid war-law model that combines features of the war model with the law model. The new war model allows the use of lethal force, the foreseen but unintended killing of innocents, and the capturing and killing of suspected terrorists. These are features of war. But in traditional war, the enemy can legitimately fight back, other nations can opt for neutrality, and enemy soldiers have certain rights under the Geneva Convention. The war on terrorism rejects these features by appealing to a law model. Terrorists are criminals, so they cannot legitimately fight back. Other nations cannot be neutral when it comes to illegal murder. If they harbor or aid terrorists, they are against us. Finally, terrorists are treated as enemy combatants rather than as soldiers or ordinary criminals, and as such, they have no rights—neither the rights of ordinary criminals nor the rights of soldiers under the Geneva Convention. There is no presumption of innocence, no right to a hearing, and they can be detained indefinitely. Even torture is allowable. So according to Luban, the war on terrorism produces an end of international human rights because anyone identified as a terrorist has no rights. (For an example of the treatment of suspected terrorists, see the case of Jose Padilla in the Problem Cases.)

Philosophical Issues

The readings in the chapter raise some very important issues. Can war be justified, and if so, how? Pacifists such as Schweitzer and Gandhi, who were opposed to all killing or all violence, hold that no war is ever justified. The problem with these absolutist views is that there seems to be an obvious exception, namely, killing or violence in the defense of one's life. Lackey's antiwar pacifism is not so easily dismissed. If one agrees that the killing of soldiers and civilians is a very great evil, one that cannot be balanced by goods such as political freedom, then it seems very difficult, if not impossible, to justify modern wars.

Just war theorists such as O'Brien try to justify modern wars such as World War II, but to do so they have to modify or interpret the principles of the theory. The most troublesome principle is the one about discrimination. As O'Brien says, if this principle is understood to forbid absolutely the killing of noncombatants, then it is hard to see how any modern war could be justified, since they all involved killing noncombatants. Perhaps the most graphic example was the atomic bombing of Hiroshima and Nagasaki, which killed over 200,000 innocent noncombatants. There are various ways to get around the problem. One is to deny that there are any innocent noncombatants in war; everyone in an enemy nation is a legitimate target. (Some terrorists take this position, too.) The most common way of justifying the killing of innocents, as we have seen, is to appeal to the Catholic doctrine of double effect.

There is debate about how to formulate and apply the doctrine of double effect. In the reading, O'Brien admits that the distinction between the two effects, one that is directly intended and the other, an unintended side effect, is often difficult to accept. Consider President Harry Truman's decision to bomb Hiroshima and Nagasaki. At the time, he said that his decision was based on the fact that an invasion of Japan would cost the lives of thousands of American soldiers, and he wanted to save those lives. But he surely knew that using atomic bombs on these undefended cities would result in the deaths of thousands of innocent Japanese noncombatants. Did he directly intend the killing of innocents or merely foresee this killing as an unintended consequence? Can we make the distinction in this case, and if we do, then what is the basis for the distinction?

Are acts of terrorism ever justified? As we have seen, Calhoun argues that terrorists can and do appeal to the just war theory, the very theory that others use to demonstrate that terrorism is wrong. How can just war theory be used to defend terrorism? Calhoun argues that terrorists can appeal to the doctrine of double effect. To see how this might be done, let's take another look at the doctrine as stated by Father Richard McCormick and quoted by O'Brien. McCormick says, "It is immoral directly to take innocent human life except with divine authorization." Why is the killing of innocents allowed if there is divine authorization? One explanation is that just war theory was developed by Catholic theologians to defend the holy crusades against infidels, crusades that were believed to be commanded by God. But of course fundamentalist Muslim terrorists also believe they have divine authorization; they believe they are engaged in a holy war commanded by Allah against infidels. Thus, both Christians and Muslims claim divine authorization for war and terrorism.

Now let us turn to the distinction between direct and indirect killing, which is at the heart of the doctrine of double effect. As McCormick explains it, "Direct taking of human life implies that one performs a lethal action with the intention that death should result for himself or another. Death is therefore deliberately willed as the effect of one's action." But Muslim terrorists may sincerely believe that all things happen by Allah's will, and they do not will anything, much less the death of others. They are merely submitting to the will of Allah, and Allah commands them to jihad. So they can claim that the deaths that result from their actions are not positively willed, but merely foreseen as a consequence of following Allah's commands. In other words, they are only indirectly killing innocents. It appears, then, that terrorists can attempt to justify their actions by appealing to the Catholic doctrine of double effect, at least as it is stated by McCormick.

How do we define terrorism? This is another issue discussed in the readings. Calhoun argues that there is no satisfactory definition of terrorism. The moral definition, which defines terrorism as killing or threatening to kill innocent people, is unsatisfactory because it seems to apply to every nation that has engaged in bombing campaigns resulting in the deaths of innocent children. The legal definition, which defines terrorism as illegal acts of killing or harming people, is defective because it would not apply to the reign of terror imposed by the Third Reich in Nazi Germany.

Richardson asserts that terrorism simply means deliberately and violently targeting civilians for political purposes. She admits that this simple definition applies to some actions of democratic states. She mentions the Allied bombing campaign in World War II, which targeted the cities in Germany, and the nuclear bombing of Hiroshima and Nagasaki. Current examples are not hard to find. In the Lebanon War, Israel used unguided cluster bombs to attack civilian targets. In 1986, the United States tried to kill Colonel Gaddafi, the Libyan leader, and succeeded in killing his fifteen-month-old daughter and fifteen other civilians. Richardson's solution to the problem of state terrorism is to stipulate, for the sake of "analytic clarity," that terrorism is the act of substate groups, not states. She adds, however, that when states deliberately target civilian populations, as they did in World War II, this is the moral equivalent of terrorism.

Card adopts Carl Wellman's definition of terrorism as political violence with two targets: a direct but secondary target that suffers the harm and an indirect but primary target that gets a political message. By this definition, the 9/11 attacks were clearly terrorist attacks. They were also evil, indeed paradigmatically evil, because the harms were intolerable, planned, and foreseeable.

Finally, how should we deal with terrorists? Do we treat them as enemy soldiers who have rights under the Geneva Convention, such as the right not to be tortured and the right to be fed, clothed, given medical treatment, and released when hostilities are over? In Card's view, terrorists should be treated as criminals, not soldiers. We should hunt down those responsible for the terrorist attacks like 9/11, including those who planned and supported the attacks. When captured, they should be charged with crimes against humanity and given an international trial. But if they are criminals, do they have the legal rights of ordinary criminals, such as the presumption of innocence, the right to a fair trial, the right to be defended by a lawyer, the right not to testify against themselves, and the right not to be held without charges? Luban argues that the war on terrorism treats suspected terrorists as neither soldiers nor criminals but as enemy combatants with no rights at all, and this amounts to the end of international human rights.

Pacifism

DOUGLAS P. LACKEY

Douglas P. Lackey is professor of philosophy at Baruch College and the Graduate Center of the City University of New York. He is the author of *Moral Principles and Nuclear Weapons* (1984), *Ethics of War and Peace* (1989), *God, Immortality, Ethics* (1990), and *Ethics and Strategic Defense* (1990). Our reading is taken from *The Ethics of War and Peace* (1989).

Lackey distinguishes between four types of pacifism. There is the universal pacifist view that all killing is wrong, the universal pacifist view that all violence is wrong, private pacifism that condemns personal violence but not political violence, and antiwar pacifism that allows personal violence but condemns all wars. Lackey discusses objections to all of these views, but he seems to defend antiwar pacifism. Or at least he answers every objection to antiwar pacifism, leaving the reader with the impression that he supports this view.

1. VARIETIES OF PACIFISM

Everyone has a vague idea of what a pacifist is, but few realize that there are many kinds of pacifists. (Sometimes the different kinds quarrel with each other!) One task for the student of international ethics is to distinguish the different types of pacifism and to identify which types represent genuine moral theories.

Most of us at some time or other have run into the "live and let live" pacifist, the person who says, "I am absolutely opposed to killing and violence—but I don't seek to impose my own code on anyone else. If other people want to use violence, so be it. They have their values and I have mine." For such a person, pacifism is one life style among others, a life style committed to gentleness and care, and opposed to belligerence and militarism. Doubtless, many people who express such commitments are sincere and are prepared to live by their beliefs. At the same time, it is important to see why "live and let live" pacifism does not constitute a moral point of view.

When someone judges that a certain action, A, is morally wrong, that judgment entails that no one should do A. Thus, there is no way to have moral values without believing that these values apply to other people. If a person says that A is morally wrong but that it doesn't matter if other people do A, than that person either is being inconsistent or doesn't know what the word "moral" means. If a person believes that killing, in certain circumstances, is morally wrong, that belief implies that no one should kill, at least in those circumstances. If a pacifist claims that killing is wrong in *all* circumstances, but that it is permissible for other people to kill on occasion, then he has not understood the universal character of genuine moral principles. If pacifism is to be a moral theory, it must be prescribed for all or prescribed for none.

Once one recognizes this "universalizing" character of genuine moral beliefs, one will take moral commitments more seriously than those who treat a moral code as a personal life-style. Since moral principles apply to everyone, we must take care that our moral principles are correct, checking that they are not inconsistent with each other, developing and adjusting them so that they are detailed and subtle enough to

Source: Douglas P. Lackey, "Pacifism" from *The Ethics of War and Peace* by Douglas P. Lackey, pp. 6–24. Prentice Hall, Inc. Copyright 1989. Electronically reproduced by permission of Pearson Education, Inc., Upper Saddle River, NJ.

deal with a variety of circumstances, and making sure that they are defensible against the objections of those who do not accept them. Of course many pacifists do take the business of morality seriously and advance pacifism as a genuine moral position, not as a mere life-style. All such serious pacifists believe that *everyone* ought to be a pacifist, and that those who reject pacifism are deluded or wicked. Moreover, they do not simply endorse pacifism; they offer arguments in its defense. *Types of Pacifism*

We will consider four types of pacifist moral theory. First, there are pacifists who maintain that the central idea of pacifism is the immorality of killing. Second, there are pacifists who maintain that the essence of pacifism is the immorality of violence, whether this be violence in personal relations or violence in relations between nation-states. Third, there are pacifists who argue that personal violence is always morally wrong but that political violence is sometimes morally right: for example, that it is sometimes morally permissible for a nation to go to war. Fourth and finally, there are pacifists who believe that personal violence is sometimes permissible but that war is always morally wrong.

Albert Schweitzer, who opposed all killing on the grounds that life is sacred, was the first sort of pacifist. Mohandas Gandhi and Leo Tolstoy, who opposed not only killing but every kind of coercion and violence, were pacifists of the second sort: I will call such pacifists "universal pacifists." St. Augustine, who condemned self-defense but endorsed wars against heretics, was a pacifist of the third sort. Let us call him a "private pacifist," since he condemned only violence in the private sphere. Pacifists of the fourth sort, increasingly common in the modern era of nuclear and total war, I will call "antiwar pacifists."

2. THE PROHIBITION AGAINST KILLING

(a) The Biblical Prohibition

One simple and common argument for pacifism is the argument that the Bible, God's revealed word, says to all people "Thou shalt not kill" (Exod. 20:13). Some pacifists interpret this

sentence as implying that no one should kill under any circumstances, unless God indicates that this command is suspended, as He did when He commanded Abraham to slay Isaac. The justification for this interpretation is the words themselves, "Thou shalt not kill," which are presented in the Bible bluntly and without qualification, not only in Exodus but also in Deuteronomy (5:17).

This argument, however, is subject to a great many criticisms. The original language of Exodus and Deuteronomy is Hebrew, and the consensus of scholarship says that the Hebrew sentence at Exodus 20:23, "Lo Tirzach," is best translated as "Thou shalt do no murder," not as "Thou shalt not kill." If this translation is correct, then Exodus 20:13 does not forbid all killing but only those killings that happen to be murders. Furthermore, there are many places in the Bible where God commands human beings to kill in specified circumstances. God announces 613 commandments in all, and these include "Thou shalt not suffer a witch to live" (Exod. 22:18); "He that blasphemeth the name of the Lord... shall surely be put to death, and all the congregation shall stone him" (Lev. 24:16); "He that killeth any man shall surely be put to death" (Lev. 24:17); and so forth. It is difficult to argue that these instructions are like God's specific instructions to Abraham to slay Isaac: these are general commandments to be applied by many people, to many people, day in and day out. They are at least as general and as divinely sanctioned as the commandment translated "Thou shalt not kill."

There are other difficulties for pacifists who pin their hopes on prohibitions in the Hebrew Bible. Even if the commandment "Thou shalt not kill," properly interpreted, did prohibit all types of killing, the skeptics can ask whether this, by itself, proves that all killing is immoral. First, how do we know that statements in the Hebrew Bible really are God's word, and not just the guesses of ancient scribes? Second, even if the commandments in the Bible do express God's views, why are we morally bound to obey divine commands? (To say that we will be punished if we do not obey is to appeal to fear and self-interest, not to moral sentiments). Third, are the commandments in the Old Testament laws for all people, or just laws for the children of Israel? If they are laws for all people, then all people who do not eat unleavened bread for Passover are either deluded or wicked. If they are laws only for the children of Israel, they are religious laws and not moral laws, since they lack the universality that all moral laws must have.

Finally, the argument assumes the existence of God, and philosophers report that the existence of God is not easy to demonstrate. Even many religious believers are more confident of the truth of basic moral judgments, such as "Small children should not be tortured to death for purposes of amusement," than they are confident of the existence of God. For such people, it would seem odd to try to justify moral principles by appeals to religious principles, since the evidence for those religious principles is weaker than the evidence for the moral principles they are supposed to justify.

(b) The Sacredness of Life

There are, however, people who oppose all killing but do not seek justification in divine revelation. Many of these defend pacifism by appeal to the sacredness of life. Almost everyone is struck with wonder when watching the movements and reactions of a newborn baby, and almost everyone can be provoked to awe by the study of living things, great and small. The complexity of the mechanisms found in living bodies, combined with the efficiency with which they fulfill their functions, is not matched by any of the processes in nonliving matter. People who are particularly awestruck by the beauty of living things infer these feelings that life is sacred, that all killing is wrong.

Different versions of pacifism have been derived from beliefs about the sacredness of life. The most extreme version forbids the killing of any living thing. This view was allegedly held by Pythagoras, and presently held by members of the Jain religion in India. (Those who think that such pacifists must soon starve to death should note that a life-sustaining diet can easily be constructed from milk, honey, fallen fruit and

vegetables, and other items that are consumable without prior killing.) A less extreme view sanctions the killing of plants but forbids the killing of animals. The most moderate view prohibits only the killing of fellow beings.

There is deep appeal in an argument that connects the sacredness of life with the wrongfulness of taking life. Even people who are not pacifists are often revolted by the spectacle of killing, and most Americans would be unable to eat meat if they had to watch how the animals whose flesh they consume had been slaughtered, or if they had to do the slaughtering themselves. Most people sense that they do not own the world they inhabit and recognize that they are not free to do with the world as they will, that the things in it, most especially living things, are worthy of respect and care. Seemingly nothing could violate the respect living things deserve more than killing, especially since much of the taking of human and nonhuman life is so obviously unnecessary.

But with the introduction of the word "unnecessary" a paradox arises. Sometimes—less often than we think, but sometimes—the taking of some lives will save other lives. Does the principle that life is sacred and ought to be preserved imply that nothing should ever be killed, or does it imply that as much life should be preserved as possible? Obviously pacifists take the former view; nonpacifists, the latter.

The view that killing is wrong because it destroys what is sacred seems to imply that killing is wrong because killing diminishes the amount of good in the world. It seems to follow that if a person can save more lives by killing than by refusing to kill, arguments about the sacredness of life would not show that killing in these circumstances is wrong. (It might be wrong for other reasons.) The more lives saved, the greater the quantity of good in the world.

The difficulty that some killing might, on balance, save lives, is not the only problem for pacifism based on the sacredness of life. If preserving life is the highest value, a value not comparable with other, non-life-preserving goods, it follows that any acts which place life at risk are immoral. But many admirable actions have been undertaken in the face of death, and many less heroic but morally impeccable actions—driving on a road at moderate speed, authorizing a commercial flight to take off, and so forth—place life at risk. In cases of martyrdom in which people choose death over religious conversion, life is just as much destroyed as it is in a common murder. Yet, on the whole, automobile drivers, air traffic controllers, and religious martyrs are not thought to be wicked. Likewise, people on life-sustaining machinery sometimes request that the machines be turned off, on the grounds that quality of life matters more than quantity of life. We may consider such people mistaken, but we hardly think that they are morally depraved.

In answering this objection, the pacifist may wish to distinguish between *killing other people* and *getting oneself killed,* arguing that only the former is immoral. But although there is a genuine distinction between killing and getting killed, the distinction does not entail that killing other people destroys life but getting oneself killed does not. If life is sacred, life, including one's own life, must be preserved at all cost. In many cases, people consider the price of preserving their own lives simply too high.

(c) The Right to Life

Some pacifists may try to avoid the difficulties of the "sacredness of life" view by arguing that the essential immorality of killing is that it violates the *right to life* that every human being possesses. If people have a right to life, then it is never morally permissible to kill some people in order to save others, since according to the usual interpretation of rights, it is never permissible to violate a right in order to secure some good.

A discussion of the logic of rights in general and the right to life in particular is beyond the scope of this book. But a number of students of this subject are prepared to argue that the possession of any right implies the permissibility of defending that right against aggression: if this were not so, what would be the point of asserting the existence of rights? But if the possession of a right to life implies the permissibility of defending that right against aggression—a defense that may require killing the aggressor—then the existence of a right to life cannot by itself imply the impermissiblity of killing. On this view, the right to life implies the right to self-defense, including violent self-defense. It does not imply pacifism.

3. UNIVERSAL PACIFISM

(a) Christian Pacifism

Universal pacifists are morally opposed to all violence, not just to killing. Many universal pacifists derive their views from the Christian Gospels. In the Sermon on the Mount, Christ taught:

> Ye have heard that it hath been said, An eye for an eye, a tooth for a tooth:
> But I say unto you, that ye resist not evil: but whosoever shall smite thee on the right cheek, turn to him the other also. . . .
> Ye have heard it said, thou shalt love thy neighbor, and hate thine enemy. But I say unto you, Love your enemies, bless them that curse you, do good to them that hate you. . . . that ye may be the children of your father which is in heaven: for he maketh the sun to rise on the evil and on the good, and sendeth the rain on the just and the unjust. (Matt, 5:38–45)

In the early centuries of the Christian era, it was widely assumed that to follow Christ and to obey His teaching meant that one should reject violence and refuse service in the Roman army. But by the fifth century, after the Roman Empire had become Christian and after barbarian Goths in 410 sacked Rome itself, Church Fathers debated whether Christ really intended that the Empire and its Church should remain undefended. The Church Fathers noticed passages in the Gospels that seem to contradict pacifism:

> Think not that I am come to send peace on earth: I came not to send peace, but a sword.
> For I am come to set a man at variance against his father, and the daughter against her mother, and the daughter-in-law against her mother-in-law. (Matt. 10:34–35)

And there are several instances in the Gospels (for instance, Matt. 8:5–10) in which Jesus encounters soldiers and does not rebuke them for engaging in an occupation that is essentially committed to violence. Rather, he argues, "Render unto Caesar the things which are Caesar's; and unto God the things that are God's" (Matt. 22:21). This would seem to include military service, or at least taxes to pay for the army.

A thorough analysis of whether the Gospels command pacifism is beyond the scope of this book. The passages in the Sermon on the Mount seem to be clearly pacifist; yet many eminent scholars have denied the pacifist message. A more interesting question, for philosophy, if not for biblical scholarship, is this: If Jesus did preach pacifism in the Sermon on the Mount, did He preach it as a *moral* doctrine?

Jesus did not view his teaching as replacing the moral law as he knew it:

> Think not that I am come to destroy the law, or the prophets: I am come not to destroy, but to fulfill....
>
> Till heaven and earth pass, one jot or one tittle shall in no wise pass from the law, till all be fulfilled. (Matt. 5:17–18)

Perhaps, then, the prescriptions of the Sermon on the Mount should be interpreted as rules that one must obey in order to follow Christ, or rules that one must follow in order to obtain salvation. But it does not follow from this alone that everyone has an obligation to follow Christ, and it does not follow from this alone that everyone has an obligation to seek salvation. Even Christians will admit that some people have refused to become Christians and have led morally admirable lives nonetheless; and if salvation is a good, one can nevertheless choose to reject it, just as a citizen can neglect to hand in a winning lottery ticket without breaking the law. If so, the prescriptions of the Sermon on the Mount apply only to Christians seeking a Christian salvation. They are not universally binding rules and do not qualify as moral principles.

(b) The Moral Exemplar Argument

Many people and at least one illustrious philosopher, Immanuel Kant, believe that morally proper action consists in choosing to act in such a way that your conduct could serve as an example for all mankind. (It was Kant's genius to recognize that moral conduct is *essentially* exemplary.) Some universal pacifists appeal to this idea, arguing that if everyone were a pacifist, the world would be a much better place than it is now. This is an argument that Leo Tolstoy (1828–1910) used to support the Gospel prescription not to resist evil:

> [Christ] put the proposition of non-resistance to evil in such a way that, according to his teaching, it was to be the foundation of the joint life of men and was to free humanity from the evil that is inflicted on itself. (*My Religion*, Ch. 4) Instead of having the whole life based on violence and every joy obtained and guarded through violence; instead of seeing each one of us punished or inflicting punishment from childhood to old age, I imagined that we were all impressed in word and deed by the idea that vengeance is a very low, animal feeling; that violence is not only a disgraceful act, but also one that deprives man of true happiness....
>
> I imagined that instead of those national hatreds which are impressed on us under the form of patriotism, instead of those glorifications of murder, called wars...that we were impressed with the idea that the recognition of any countries, special laws, borders, lands, is a sign of grossest ignorance....
>
> Through the fulfillment of these commandments, the life of men will be what every human heart seeks and desires. All men will be brothers and everybody will always be at peace with others, enjoying all the benefits of the world. (*My Religion*, Ch. 6)

Few would deny that if everyone were a pacifist, the world would be a better place, perhaps even a paradise. Furthermore, since the argument is essentially hypothetical, it cannot be refuted (as many nonpacifists believe) by pointing out that not everyone will become a pacifist. The problem is whether this argument can establish pacifism as a moral imperative.

One difficulty with the argument is that it seems to rely on a premise the truth of which is purely verbal. In what way would the world be a better place if people gave up fighting?

The most obvious way is that the world would be better because there would be no war. But the statement "If everyone gave up fighting, there would be no war" is true by definition, since "war" implies "fighting." It is difficult to see how a statement that simply relates the meanings of words could tell us something about our moral obligations.

A deeper problem with Tolstoy's argument is that "resist not evil" is not the only rule that would yield paradise if everyone obeyed it. Suppose that everyone in the world subscribed to the principle "Use violence, but only in self-defense." If everyone used violence only in self-defense, the same consequences would follow as would arise from universal acceptance of the rule "Never use violence." Consequently, pacifism cannot be shown to be superior to nonpacifism by noting the good consequences that would undeniably ensue if everyone were a pacifist.

(c) Gandhian Pacifism

Certainly the most interesting and effective pacifist of the twentieth century was Mohandas Gandhi (1869–1948). Though a devout Hindu, Gandhi developed his doctrine of nonviolence from elementary metaphysical concepts that are by no means special to Hinduism:

> Man as an animal is violent, but as spirit, nonviolent. The moment he awakes to the spirit he cannot remain violent. Either he progresses towards *ahimsa* [nonviolence] or rushes to his doom. (*Nonviolence in Peace and War*, I, p. 311)

The requirement not to be violent seems wholly negative; sleeping people achieve it with ease. But for Gandhi the essential moral task is not merely to be nonviolent but to use the force of the soul (*satyagraha*, "truth grasping") in a continual struggle for justice. The methods of applied *satyagraha* developed by Gandhi— the weaponless marches, the sit-downs and sit-ins, strikes and boycotts, fasts and prayers— captured the admiration of the world and have been widely copied, most notably by Martin Luther King, Jr., in his campaigns against racial discrimination. According to Gandhi, each person, by engaging in *satyagraha* and experiencing suffering on behalf of justice, purifies the soul from pollution emanating from man's animal nature:

> A *satyagrahi* is dead to his body even before his enemy attempts to kill him, i.e. he is free from the attachments of his body and lives only in the victory of his soul. (*Nonviolence in Peace and War*, I, p. 318) Nonviolence implies as complete self-purification as is humanly possible. (*Nonviolence in Peace and War*, I, p. 111)

By acting nonviolently, pacifists not only purify their own souls but also transform the souls of their opponents: "A nonviolent revolution is not a program of seizure of power. It is a program of transformation of relationships, ending in peaceful transfer of power" (*Nonviolence in Peace and War*, II, p. 8)

Though in most places Gandhi emphasizes the personal redemption that is possible only through nonviolent resistance to evil, the spiritually positive effect of nonviolence on evil opponents is perhaps equally important, since "The soul of the *satagrahi* is love" (*Nonviolence in Peace and War*, II, p. 59).

Gandhi, then, is far from preaching the sacredness of biological life. What matters is not biological life but the condition of the soul, the natural and proper state of which is *ahimsa*. The evil of violence is that it distorts and disrupts this natural condition of the soul. The basic moral law (*dharma*) for all people is to seek the restoration of their souls to the harmony of *ahimsa*. This spiritual restoration cannot be achieved by violence, but only by the application of *satyagraha*. Disharmony cannot produce harmony; violence cannot produce spiritual peace.

The "sacredness of life" defense of pacifism ran into difficulties analyzing situations in which taking one life could save many lives. For Gandhi, this is no problem at all: taking one life may save many biological lives, but it will not save souls. On the contrary, the soul of the killer will be perverted by the act, and that perversion—not the loss of life—is what matters morally.

The system of values professed by Gandhi— that the highest human good is a harmonious condition of soul—must be kept in mind when considering the frequent accusation that Gandhi's method of nonviolent resistance "does not work," that nonviolence alone did not and could not force the British to leave India, and that nonviolent resistance to murderous tyrants like Hitler will only provoke the mass murder of the innocent. Perhaps the practice of nonviolence could not "defeat" the British or "defeat" Hitler, but by Gandhi's standard the use of military force would only produce a greater defeat, perverting the souls of thousands engaged in war and intensifying the will to violence on the opposing side. On the other hand, the soul of the *satyagrahi* will be strengthened and purified by nonviolent struggle against British imperialism or German Nazism, and in this purification the Gandhian pacifist can obtain spiritual victory even in the face of political defeat.

India did not adopt the creed of nonviolence after the British left in 1948, and it is hardly likely that any modern nation-state will organize its international affairs along Gandhian lines. But none of this affects the validity of Gandhi's arguments, which indicate how things ought to be, not how they are. We have seen that Gandhi's principles do not falter in the face of situations in which taking one life can save lives on balance. But what of situations in which the sacrifice of spiritual purity by one will prevent the corruption of many souls? Suppose, for example, that a Gandhian believes (on good evidence) that a well-timed commando raid will prevent a nation from embarking on an aggressive war, a war that would inflame whole populations with hatred for the enemy. Wouldn't a concern with one's own spiritual purity in such a situation show an immoral lack of concern for the souls of one's fellow men?

Another problem for Gandhi concerns the relationship between violence and coercion. To coerce people is to make them act against their will, for fear of the consequences they will suffer if they do not obey. Coercion, then, is a kind of spiritual violence, directed against the imagination and will of the victim. The "violence" most conspicuously rejected by Gandhi—pushing, shoving, striking with hands, the use of weapons, the placing of bombs and explosives—is essentially physical violence, directed against the bodies of opponents. But if physical violence against bodies is spiritually corrupting, psychological violence directed at the will of opponents must be even more corrupting.

In his writings Gandhi condemned coercion. Yet in practice he can hardly be said to have renounced *psychological* coercion. Obviously he would have preferred to have the British depart from India of their own free will, deciding that it was in their own best interest, or at least morally necessary, to leave. But if the British had decided, in the absence of coercion, to stay, Gandhi was prepared to exert every kind of nonviolent pressure to make them go. And when Gandhi on occasion attempted to achieve political objectives by a "fast unto death," his threat of self-starvation brought enormous psychological pressure on the authorities, who, among other things, feared the riots would ensue should Gandhi die.

The Gandhian pacifist, then, must explain why psychological pressure is permissible if physical pressure is forbidden. One possible answer is that physical pressure cannot transform the soul of the opponents, but psychological pressure, since it operates on the mind, can effect a spiritual transformation. Indeed, Gandhi characterized his terrifying fasts as acts of education, not coercion. But the claim that these fasts were not coercive confuses the noncoercive intention behind the act with its predictable coercive effects; and if education is the name of the game, the nonpacifists will remark that violence has been known to teach a few good lessons in its day. In many spiritual traditions, what matters essentially is not the kind of pressure but that the right pressure be applied at the right time and in the right way. Zen masters have brought students to enlightenment by clouting them on the ears, and God helped St. Paul to see the light by knocking him off his horse.

In addition to these technical problems, many people will be inclined to reject the system of values from which Gandhi's deductions flow. Many will concede that good character is important and that helping others to develop moral virtues is an important task. But few agree with Gandhi that the development of moral purity is the supreme human good, and that other goods, like the preservation of human life, or progress in the arts and sciences, have little or no value in comparison. If even a little value is conceded to these other things, then on occasion it will be necessary to put aside the project of developing spiritual purity in order to preserve other values. These acts of preservation may require physical violence, and those who use violence to defend life or beauty or liberty may indeed be corrupting their souls. But it is hard to believe that an occasional and necessary act of violence on behalf of these values will totally and permanently corrupt the soul, and those who use violence judiciously may be right in thinking that the saving of life or beauty or liberty may be worth a small or temporary spiritual loss.

4. PRIVATE PACIFISM

Perhaps the rarest form of pacifist is the pacifist who renounces violence in personal relations but condones the use of force in the political sphere. Such a pacifist will not use violence for self-defense but believes that it is permissible for the state to use judicial force against criminals and military force against foreign enemies. A private pacifist renounces self-defense but supports national defense.

(a) Augustine's Limited Pacifism

Historically, private pacifism developed as an attempt to reconcile the demands of the Sermon on the Mount with the Christian duty to charity. The Sermon on the Mount requires Christians to "resist not evil"; the duty of charity requires pity for the weak who suffer the injustice of the strong. For St. Augustine (354–430), one essential message of the Gospels is the good news that this present life is as nothing compared with the life to come. The person who tries to hold on to earthly possessions is deluded as to what is truly valuable: "If any man will sue thee at the law, and take away thy coat, let him have thy cloak also" (Matt. 5:40). What goes for earthly coats should go for earthly life as well, so if any man seeks to take a Christian life, the Christian should let him have it. On this view, the doctrine "resist no evil" is just an expression of contempt for earthly possessions.

But according to Augustine there are some things in this world that do have value: justice, for example, the relief of suffering, and the preservation of the Church, which Augustine equated with civilization itself. To defend these things with necessary force is not to fall prey to delusions about the good. For Augustine, then, service in the armed forces is not inconsistent with Christian values.

One difficulty for theories like Augustine's is that they seem to justify military service only when military force is used in a just cause. Unfortunately, once in the service, the man in the ranks is not in a position to evaluate the justice of his nation's cause; indeed, in many modern nations, the principle of military subordination to civilian rule prevents even generals from evaluating the purposes of war declared by political leaders. But Augustine argues that the cause of justice cannot be served without armies, and armies cannot function unless subordinates follow orders without questioning the purposes of the conflict. The necessary conditions for justice and charity require that some men put themselves in positions in which they might be required to fight for injustice.

(b) The Problem of Self-Defense

Many will agree with Augustine that most violence at the personal level—the violence of crime, vendetta, and domestic brutality, for example—goes contrary to moral principles. But most are prepared to draw the line at personal and collective self-defense. Can the obligation to be charitable justify participation in military service but stop short of justifying the use of force by private citizens, if that force is exercised to protect the weak from the oppression of the strong? Furthermore, the obligation to be charitable does not exclude acts of charity toward oneself. For Augustine, violence was a dangerous tool, best kept out of the hands of the citizens and best left strictly at the disposal of the state. Beset with fears of crime in the streets, the contemporary American is less inclined to worry about the anarchic effects of private uses of defensive force and more inclined to worry about the protection the police seem unable to provide.

For these worried people, the existence of a right to self-defense is self-evident. But the existence of this right is not self-evident to universal or private pacifists; and it was not self-evident to St. Augustine. In the Christian tradition, no right to self-defense was recognized until its existence was certified by Thomas Aquinas in the thirteenth century. Aquinas derived the right to self-defense from the universal tendency to self-preservation, assuming (contrary to Augustine) that a natural tendency must be morally right. As for the Christian duty to love one's enemy, Aquinas argued that acts of self-defense have two effects—the saving of life and the taking of life—and that self-defensive uses of force intend primarily the saving of life. This makes the use of force in self-defense a morally permissible act of charity. The right to self-defense is now generally recognized in Catholic moral theology and in Western legal systems. But it can hardly be said that Aquinas's arguments, which rely heavily on assumptions from Greek philosophy, succeed in reconciling the claims of self-defense with the prescriptions of the Sermon on the Mount.

5. ANTIWAR PACIFISM

Most people who believe in the right to personal self-defense also believe that some wars are morally justified. In fact, the notion of self-defense and the notion of just war are commonly linked; just wars are said to be defensive wars, and the justice of defensive war is inferred from the right of personal self-defense, projected from the individual to the national level. But some people reject this projection: they endorse the validity of personal self-defense, but they deny that war can be justified by appeal to self-defense or any other right. On the contrary, they argue that war always involves an inexcusable violation of rights. For such anti-war pacifists, all participation in war is morally wrong.

The Killing of Soldiers

One universal and necessary feature of wars is that soldiers get killed in them. Most people accept such killings as a necessary evil, and judge the killing of soldiers in war to be morally acceptable. If the war is fought for the just cause, the killing of enemy soldiers is justified as necessary to the triumph of right. If the war is fought for an unjust cause, the killing of enemy soldiers is acceptable because it is considered an honorable thing to fight for one's country, right or wrong, provided that one fights well and cleanly. But the antiwar pacifist does not take the killing of soldiers for granted. Everyone has a right to life, and the killing of soldiers in war is intentional killing, a deliberate violation of the right to life. According to the standard interpretation of basic rights, it is never morally justifiable to violate a basic right in order to produce some good; the end, in such cases, does not justify the means. How, then, can the killing of soldiers in war be morally justified—or even excused?

Perhaps the commonest reply to the challenge of antiwar pacifism is that killing in war is a matter of self-defense, *personal* self-defense, the right to which is freely acknowledged by the antiwar pacifist. In war, the argument goes, it is either kill or be killed—and that type of killing is killing in self-defense. But though the appeal to self-defense is natural, antiwar pacifists believe that it is not successful. First of all, on the usual understanding of "self-defense," those who kill can claim the justification of self-defense only if (a) they had no other way to save their lives or preserve themselves from physical harm except by killing, and (b) they did nothing to provoke the attack to which they are subjected. Antiwar pacifists point out that soldiers on the battlefield do have a way of saving themselves from death or harm without killing anyone: they can surrender. Furthermore, for soldiers fighting for an unjust cause—for example, German soldiers fighting in the invasion of Russia in 1941—it is difficult to argue that they "did nothing to provoke" the deadly force directed at them. But if the German army provoked the Russians to stand and fight on Russian soil, German soldiers cannot legitimately claim self-defense as a moral justification for killing Russian soldiers.

To the nonpacifist, these points might seem like legalistic quibbles. But the antiwar pacifist has an even stronger argument against killing soldiers in war. The vast majority of soldiers who die in war do not die in "kill or be killed" situations. They are killed by bullets, shells, or bombs directed from safe launching points—"safe" in the sense that those who shoot the bullets or fire the shells or drop the bombs are in no immediate danger of death. Since those who kill are not in immediate danger of death, they cannot invoke "self-defense" to justify the deaths they cause.

Some other argument besides self-defense, then, must explain why the killing of soldiers in war should not be classified as murder. Frequently, nonpacifists argue that the explanation is found in the doctrine of "assumption of risk," the idea, common in civil law, that persons who freely assume a risk have only themselves to blame if the risk is realized. When a soldier goes to war, he is well aware that one risk of his trade is getting killed on the battlefield. If he dies on the field, the responsibility for his death lies with himself, not with the man who shot him. By assuming the risk—so the argument goes—he waived his right to life, at least on the battlefield.

One does not have to be a pacifist to see difficulties in this argument. First of all, in all substantial modern wars, most of the men on the line are not volunteers, but draftees. Only a wealthy nation like the United States can afford an all-volunteer army, and most experts believe that the American volunteer ranks will have to be supplemented by draftees should the United States become involved in another conflict on the scale of Korea or Vietnam. Second, in many cases in which a risk is realized, responsibility for the bad outcome lies not with the person who assumed the risk but with the person who created it. If an arsonist sets fire to a house and a parent rushes in to save the children, dying in the rescue attempt, responsibility for the parent's death lies not with the parent who assumed the risk, but with the arsonist who created it. So if German armies invade Russia, posing the risk of death in battle, and if Russian soldiers assume this risk and fight back, the deaths of Russians are the fault of German invaders, not the fault of the defenders who assumed the risk.

These criticisms of German foot soldiers will irritate many who served in the armed forces and who know how little political and military decision making is left to the men on the front lines, who seem to be the special target of these pacifist arguments. But antiwar pacifists will deny that their aim is to condemn the men on the battlefield. Most antiwar pacifists feel that soldiers in war act under considerable compulsion and are excused for that reason from responsibility for the killing they do. But to say that battlefield killings are *excusable* is not to say that they are morally *justified*. On the contrary, if such killings are excusable, it must be that there is some immorality to be excused.

The Killing of Civilians

In the chronicles of ancient wars, conflict was total and loss in battle was frequently followed by general slaughter of men, women, and children on the losing side. It has always been considered part of the trend toward civilization to confine the destruction of war to the personnel and instruments of war, sparing civilians and their property as much as possible. This civilizing trend was conspicuously reversed in World War II, in which the ratio of civilian deaths to total war deaths was perhaps the highest it had been since the wars of religion in the seventeenth century. A very high ratio of civilian deaths to total deaths was also characteristic of the war in Vietnam. Given the immense firepower of modern weapons and the great distances between the discharges of weapons and the explosions of bullets or shells near the targets, substantial civilian casualties are an inevitable part of modern land war. But it is immoral to kill civilians, the antiwar pacifist argues, and from this it follows that modern land warfare is necessarily immoral.

Few nonpacifists will argue that killing enemy civilians is justifiable when such killings are avoidable. Few will argue that killing enemy civilians is justifiable when such killings are the *primary* objective of a military operation. But what about the deaths of civilians that are the unavoidable results of military operations directed to some *other* result? The pacifist classifies such killings as immoral, whereas most non-pacifists call them regrettable but unavoidable deaths, not murders. But why are they not murder, if the civilians are innocent, and if it is known in advance that some civilians will be killed? Isn't this an intentional killing of the innocent, which is the traditional definition of murder?

The sophisticated nonpacifist may try to parry this thrust with analogies to policies outside the arena of war. There are, after all, many morally acceptable policies that, when adopted, have the effect of killing innocent persons. If the Congress decides to set a speed limit of 55 miles per hour on federal highways, more people will die than if Congress sets the speed limit at 45 miles per hour. Since many people who die on the highway are innocent, the Congress has chosen a policy that knowingly brings death to the innocent, but no one calls it murder. Or suppose, for example, that a public health officer is considering a national vaccination program to forestall a flu epidemic. He knows that if he does not implement the vaccination program, many people will die from the flu. On the other hand, if the program is implemented, a certain number of people will die of allergic reactions to the vaccine. Most of the people who die from allergic reactions will be people who would not have died of the flu if the vaccination program had not been implemented. So the vaccination program will kill innocent people who would otherwise be saved if the program were abandoned. If the public health officer implements such a program, we do *not* think that he is a murderer.

Nonpacifists argue that what makes the action of Congress and the action of the public health officer morally permissible in these cases is that the deaths of the innocent, although foreseen, are not the intended goal of these policies. Congress does not want people to die on the highways; every highway death is a regrettable death. The purpose of setting the speed limit at 55 miles per hour is not to kill people but to provide a reasonable balance between safety and convenience. Likewise, it is not the purpose of the public health officer to kill people by giving them vaccine. His goal is to save lives on balance, and every death from the vaccine is a regrettable death. Likewise, in war, when civilians are killed as a result of necessary military operations, the deaths of the civilians are not the intended goal of the military operation. They are foreseen, but they are always regretted. If we do not accuse Congress of murder and the Public Health Service of murder in these cases, consistency requires that we not accuse military forces of murder when they cause civilian deaths in war, especially if every attempt is made to keep civilian deaths to a minimum.

Antiwar pacifists do not condemn the Congress and the Public Health Service in cases like these. But they assert that the case of war is different in a morally relevant way. To demonstrate the difference, antiwar pacifists provide an entirely different analysis of the moral justification for speed limits and vaccination programs. In their opinion, the facts that highway deaths and vaccination deaths are "unintended" and "regretted" is morally irrelevant. The real justification lies in the factor of consent. In the case of federal highway regulations, the rules are decided by Congress, which is elected by the people, the same people who use the highways. If Congress decides on a 55-mile-an-hour limit, this is a regulation that, in some sense, highway drivers have imposed upon themselves. Those people who die on the highway because of a higher speed limit have, in a double sense, assumed the risks generated by that speed limit: they have, through the Congress, created the risk, and by venturing onto the highway, have freely exposed themselves to the risk. The responsibility for these highway deaths, then, lies either on the drivers themselves or on the people who crashed into them—not on the Congress.

Likewise, in the case of the vaccination program, if people are warned in advance of the risks of vaccination, and if they nevertheless choose to be vaccinated, they are responsible for their own deaths should the risks be realized. According to the antiwar pacifist, it is this consent given by drivers and vaccination volunteers that justifies these policies, and it is precisely this element of consent that is absent in the case of the risks inflicted on enemy civilians in time of war.

Consider the standard textbook example of allegedly justifiable killing of civilians in time of war. Suppose that the destruction of a certain bridge is an important military objective, but if the bridge is bombed, it is very likely that civilians living close by will be killed. (The civilians cannot be warned without alerting the enemy to reinforce the bridge.) If the bridge is bombed and some civilians are killed, the bombing victims are not in the same moral category as highway victims or victims of vaccination. The bombing victims did not order the bombing of themselves through some set of elected representatives. Nor did the bombing victims freely consent to the bombing of their bridge. Nor was the bombing in any way undertaken as a calculated risk in the interest of the victims. For all these reasons, the moral conclusions regarding highway legislation and vaccination programs do not carry over to bombing of the bridge.

Nonpacifists who recognize that it will be very difficult to fight wars without bombing bridges may argue that the victims of this bombing in some sense assumed the risks of bombardment by choosing to live close to a potential military target. Indeed, it is occasionally claimed that all the civilians in a nation at war have assumed the risks of war, since they could avoid the risks of war simply by moving to a neutral country. But such arguments are strained and uncharitable, even for those rare warring nations that permit freedom of emigration. Most people consider it a major sacrifice to give up their homes, and an option that requires such a sacrifice cannot be considered an option open for free choice. The analogy between the unintended victims of vaccination and the unintended civilian victims of war seems to have broken down.

(c) The Balance of Good and Evil in War

It is left to the nonpacifist to argue that the killing of soldiers and civilians in war is in the end justifiable in order to obtain great moral goods that can be obtained only by fighting for them. Civilians have rights to life, but those rights can be outweighed by the national objectives, provided those objectives are morally acceptable and overwhelmingly important. Admittedly, this argument for killing civilians is available only to the just side in a war, but if the argument is valid, it proves that there can *be* a just side, contrary to the arguments of antiwar pacifism.

Antiwar pacifists have two lines of defense. First, they can continue to maintain that the end does not justify the means, if the means be murderous. Second, they can, and will, go on to argue that it is a tragic mistake to believe that there are great moral goods that can be obtained only by war. According to antiwar pacifists, the amount of moral good produced by war is greatly exaggerated. The Mexican War, for example, resulted in half of Mexico being transferred to American rule. This was a great good for the United States, but not a great moral good, since the United States had little claim to the ceded territory, and no great injustice would have persisted if the war had not been fought at all.

The Revolutionary War in America is widely viewed as a war that produced a great moral good; but if the war had not been fought, the history of the United States would be similar to the history of Canada (which remained loyal)—and no one feels that the Canadians have suffered or are suffering great injustices that the American colonies avoided by war. Likewise, it is difficult to establish the goods produced by World War I or the moral losses that would have ensued if the winning side, "our side," had lost. Bertrand Russell imagined the results of a British loss in World War I as follows:

> The greatest sum that foreigners could possibly exact would be the total economic rent of the land and natural resources of England. [But] the working classes, the shopkeepers, manufacturers, and merchants, the literary men and men of science—all the people that make England of any account in the world—have at most an infinitesimal and accidental share in the rental of England. The men who have a share use

their rents in luxury, political corruption, taking the lives of birds, and depopulating and enslaving the rural districts. It is this life of the idle rich that would be curtailed if the Germans exacted tribute from England. (*Justice in War Time,* pp. 48–49)

But multiplying examples of wars that did little moral good will not establish the pacifist case. The pacifist must show that *no* war has done enough good to justify the killing of soldiers and the killing of civilians that occurred in the war. A single war that produces moral goods sufficient to justify its killings will refute the pacifist claim that *all* wars are morally unjustifiable. Obviously this brings the antiwar pacifist head to head with World War II.

It is commonly estimated that 35 million people died as a result of World War II. It is difficult to imagine that any cause could justify so much death, but fortunately the Allies need only justify their share of these killings. Between 1939 and 1945 Allied forces killed about 5.5 million Axis soldiers and about 1 million civilians in Axis countries. Suppose that Britain and the United States had chosen to stay out of World War II and suppose Stalin had, like Lenin, surrendered to Germany shortly after the invasion. Does avoiding the world that would have resulted from these decisions justify killing 6.5 million people?

If Hitler and Tojo had won the war, doubtless they would have killed a great many people both before and after victory, but it is quite likely that the total of *additional* victims, beyond those they killed in the war that *was* fought, would have been less than 6.5 million and, at any rate, the responsibility for those deaths would fall on Hitler and Tojo, not on Allied nations. If Hitler and Tojo had won the war, large portions of the world would have fallen under foreign domination, perhaps for a very long time. But the antiwar pacifist will point out that the main areas of Axis foreign domination—China and Russia—were not places in which the citizens enjoyed a high level of freedom *before the war began.* Perhaps the majority of people in the conquered areas

would have worked out a *modus vivendi* with their new rulers, as did the majority of French citizens during the German occupation. Nor can it be argued that World War II was necessary to save six million Jews from annihilation in the Holocaust, since in fact the war did *not* save them. But it saved those that would have been killed

The ultimate aims of Axis leaders are a matter for historical debate. Clearly the Japanese had no intention of conquering the United States, and some historians suggest that Hitler hoped to avoid war with England and America, declaring war with England reluctantly, and only after the English declared it against him. Nevertheless, popular opinion holds that Hitler intended to conquer the world, and if preventing the conquest of Russia and China could not justify six and one-half million killings, most Americans are quite confident that preventing the conquest of England and the United States does justify killing on this scale.

The antiwar pacifist disagrees. Certainly German rule of England and the United States would have been a very bad thing. At the same time, hatred of such German rule would be particularly fueled by hatred of foreigners, and hatred of foreigners, as such, is an irrational and morally unjustifiable passion. After all, if rule by foreigners were, by itself, a great moral wrong, the British, with their great colonial empire, could hardly consider themselves the morally superior side in World War II.

No one denies that a Nazi victory in World War II would have had morally frightful results. But, according to antiwar pacifism, killing six and one-half million people is also morally frightful, and preventing one moral wrong does not obviously outweigh committing the other. Very few people today share the pacifists' condemnation of World War II, but perhaps that is because the dead killed by the Allies cannot speak up and make sure that their losses are properly counted on the moral scales. Antiwar pacifists speak on behalf of the enemy dead, and on behalf of all those millions who would have lived if the war had not been fought. On this silent constituency they rest their moral case.

REVIEW QUESTIONS

1. Characterize universal pacifists (there are two types), private pacifists, and antiwar pacifists.
2. Why doesn't Lackey accept the appeal to the Bible, or the sacredness of life, or the right to life as a good reason for accepting pacifism?
3. What is Christian pacifism and Tolstoy's argument used to defend it? Why doesn't Lackey accept Tolstoy's argument?
4. Explain Gandhi's pacifism, including *satyagraha*. What problems does Lackey raise for this view?
5. Explain Augustine's so-called limited pacifism. What problems does this view have according to Lackey?
6. State the position of antiwar pacifism. Why do antiwar pacifists believe that all wars are wrong? According to Lackey, what are the objections to antiwar pacifism, and how can antiwar pacifists reply?

DISCUSSION QUESTIONS

1. Is Gandhi's view a defensible one? Why or why not?
2. Does the antiwar pacifist have a good reply to all the objections Lackey discusses? Are there any good objections that he does not discuss?
3. Many people think that World War II was morally justified. What does the antiwar pacifist say? What do you think?
4. According to Lackey, no great moral good was produced by the Revolutionary War in America. If America had lost this war and remained under British rule, then its history would be like that of Canada—and Canada has not suffered, he says. Do you agree? Explain your answer.

The Conduct of Just and Limited War

WILLIAM V. O'BRIEN

William V. O'Brien (1924–2003) was professor of government at Georgetown University, Washington, D.C. He is the author of *War and/or Survival* (1969), *Nuclear War, Deterrence and Morality* (1967), *The Nuclear Dilemma and the Just War Tradition* (1986), and *Law and Morality in Israel's War with the PLO* (1991). Our reading is taken from *The Conduct of Just and Limited War* (1981).

O'Brien divides just war theory into two parts. The first, *jus ad bellum,* states conditions that should be met for a state to have the right to go to war. The second, *jus in bello,* gives principles limiting conduct in war. There are three main conditions of *jus ad bellum*: The war must be declared by a competent authority for a public purpose; there must be a just cause; and there must be a right intention that aims at peace. The condition of just cause is subdivided into four more conditions: the substance of the cause (e.g., self-defense), the form of the cause (defensive or offensive), the requirement of proportionality (the good achieved by war must be proportionate to the evil of war), and peaceful means of avoiding war must be exhausted.

The *jus in bello* has two principles limiting conduct in war. The principle of proportion requires that the discrete military means and ends be balanced. The principle of discrimination prohibits the intentional attacks on noncombatants and nonmilitary targets.

The original Just-War doctrine of St. Augustine, St. Thomas, and other Scholastics emphasized the conditions for permissible recourse to war—the *jus ad bellum*. To this doctrine was added another branch of prescriptions regulating the conduct of war, the *jus in bello*. . . .

The *jus ad bellum* lays down conditions that must be met in order to have permissible recourse to armed coercion. They are conditions that should be viewed in the light of the fundamental tenet of just-war doctrine: the presumption is always against war. The taking of human life is not permitted to man unless there are exceptional justifications. Just-war doctrine provides those justifications, but they are in the nature of special pleadings to overcome the presumption against killing. The decision to invoke the exceptional rights of war must be based on the following criteria: there must be competent authority to order the war for a public purpose; there must be a just cause (it may be self-defense or the protection of rights by offensive war) and the means must be proportionate to the just cause and all peaceful alternatives must have been exhausted; and there must be right intention on the part of the just belligerent. Let us examine these criteria.

Insofar as large-scale, conventional war is concerned, the issue of competent authority is different in modern times than it was in the thirteenth century. The decentralized political system wherein public, private, and criminal violence overlapped, as well as the state of military art and science, permitted a variety of private wars. So it was important to insist that war—in which individuals would be called upon to take human lives—must be waged on the order of public authorities for public purposes. This is not a serious problem in most parts of the world today. Only states have the material capacity to wage large-scale, modern, conventional war. Two other problems do, however, exist in connection with the conditions of competent authority. First, there may be disputes as to the constitutional competence of a particular official or organ of state to initiate war. Second, civil war and revolutionary terrorism are frequently initiated by persons and organizations claiming revolutionary rights.

Most states today, even totalitarian states, have specific constitutional provisions for the declaration and termination of war. If an official or state organ violates these provisions, there may not be a valid exercise of the sovereign right to declare and wage war. In such a case the first condition of the just war might not be met. This was the charge, implicitly or explicitly, against President Johnson in the Vietnam War. Johnson never requested a declaration of war from Congress with which he shared war-making powers. War critics asserted that the undeclared war was illegal. A sufficient answer to this charge is to be found in congressional cooperation in the war effort and in the refusal of the courts to declare the war unconstitutional. . . . At this point it is sufficient to raise the issue as illustrative of the problem of competent authority within a constitutional state.

In this connection a word should be said about declaring wars. Any examination of modern wars will show that the importance of a declaration of war has diminished greatly in international practice. Because of the split-second timing of modern war, it is often undesirable to warn the enemy by way of a formal declaration. Defense measures are geared to react to hostile behavior, not declarations. When war is declared it is often an announcement confirming a condition that has already been established. Nevertheless, if a particular state's constitution does require a formal declaration of war and one is not forthcoming, the issue of competence is raised. If a public official exceeds his authority in mobilizing the people and conducting war, there is a lack of competent authority.

The second problem, however, is by far the greatest. Today, rights of revolution are frequently invoked by organizations and individuals. They clearly do not have the authority and capacity to wage war in the conventional sense. However, they do wage revolutionary war, often on an international scale. Indeed, international terrorism is one of the most pervasive and difficult problems facing the international community.

All major ideologies and blocs or alignments of states in the international system recognize the right of revolution. Usually their interpretations will emphasize the rights of revolution against others, not themselves.... Logically, there should be an elaborate *jus ad bellum* and *jus in bello* for revolutionary war, but development of such a doctrine has never been seriously attempted. As a result, the issues of revolutionary war tend to be treated on an ad hoc basis as special cases vaguely related to the regular categories of just war....

The differences between conventional war waged by states and revolutionary war waged by rebels against states are profound. Given the formidable power of most modern governments, particularly in regard to their comparative monopoly of armed force, revolutionary rights can be asserted mainly by covert organizations waging guerrilla warfare and terrorism. The option of organizing a portion of a state and fighting a conventional civil war in the manner of the American, Spanish, or Nigerian civil wars is seldom available.

The covert, secret character of modern revolutionary movements is such that it is often hard to judge their claims to qualify as the competent authority for oppressed people. There is a decided tendency to follow the Leninist model of revolutionary leadership wherein the self-selected revolutionary elite decides on the just revolutionary cause, the means, and the circumstances of taking the initiative, all done in the name of the people and revolutionary justice. As a revolution progresses, the task of certifying competent authority continues to be difficult. Support for the revolutionary leadership is often coerced or given under conditions where there is not popular acceptance of the revolutionary authority of that leadership or its ends and means. Recognition by foreign powers of belligerency—or even of putative governmental powers—is an unreliable guide given subjective, politicized recognition policies.

To complicate matters, individuals and small groups take up revolutionary war tactics, principally terrorism in the form of airplane hijacking, hostage kidnapping, assassination, and indiscriminate bombing attacks. These acts are performed in the name of greatly varying causes, some of which could not be considered revolutionary. Sometimes the alleged justifications are political or ideological, but, on investigation, the real motivation turns out to be personal and criminal. Since most revolutionary movements manifest themselves in behavior difficult to distinguish from that of cranks and criminals, the task of sorting out revolutionaries entitled to acceptance as competent authorities is excruciating.

Two issues need to be resolved concerning revolutionary activity. First, insofar as treating revolutionaries as belligerents in a war and not as common criminals is concerned, the ultimate answer lies in the character, magnitude, and degree of success of the revolutionaries. If they can organize a government that carries on their war in a controlled fashion (assuming a magnitude requiring countermeasures that more resemble war than ordinary police operations), and if the conflict continues for an appreciable time, the revolutionaries may have won their right to be considered a competent authority for purposes of just war. Beyond this enumeration of criteria it seems unprofitable to generalize.

Second, concerning the authority of rebel leaders to mobilize the people by ordering or coercing individuals to fight for the revolutionary cause, the conscience of the individual takes precedence. Lacking any color of authority to govern, the rebels cannot of right compel participation in their cause. Needless to say, they will very probably compel participation by intimidation.

JUST CAUSE

...Authorities vary in their presentation of just cause, but it seems to break down into four subdivisions: the substance of the just cause, the forms of pursuing just cause, the requirement of proportionality of ends and means, and the requirement of exhaustion of peaceful remedies.

The substance of the just cause must, in Childress's formulation, be sufficiently "serious and weighty" to overcome the presumption of killing in general and war in particular. In Childress's approach, with which I am in essential agreement, this means that there must be a "competing prima facie duty or obligation" to "the prima facie obligation not to injure or kill others."[1] Childress mentions as "serious and weighty" prima facie obligations the following: (1) "to protect the innocent from unjust attack," (2) "to restore rights wrongfully denied," (3) "to reestablish a just order."

This is an adequate basis, reflective of the older just-war literature, for discussing the substance of just cause. Indeed, Childress is more explicit than many modern commentators who simply state that there should be a just cause. Still, it is only a beginning. It is unfortunate that modern moralists have generally been so concerned with the issue of putatively disproportionate means of modern war that they have neglected the prior question of the ends for which these means might have to be used (that is, just cause). In practical terms, this task of evaluating the substance of just cause leads inescapably to a comparative analysis of the characteristics of the polities or political-social systems posed in warlike confrontation. . . .

Even more difficult for those who would answer in the affirmative is the question whether the United States should intervene to protect a manifestly imperfect political-social order (South Korea, South Vietnam or, perhaps, that of a state such as Jordan, Saudi Arabia, or Pakistan). . . .

By comparison, the substantive just causes of the older just-war literature are almost insignificant. In the modern world the just cause often has to do with the survival of a way of life. Claims that this is so can be false or exaggerated, but they are often all too legitimate. They must be taken seriously in assessing the substance of just cause in modern just-war analyses.

However, passing the test of just cause is not solely a matter of positing an end that is convincingly just, although that is the indispensable starting point. It is also necessary to meet the tests posed by the other three subdivisions of just cause.

The forms of pursuing just cause are defensive and offensive wars. The justice of self-defense is generally considered to be axiomatic. Just-war doctrine, following Aristotle and St. Thomas as well as the later Scholastics, places great importance on the state as a natural institution essential for man's development. Defense of the state is prima facie of an essential social institution. So strong is the presumption in favor of the right of self-defense that the requirement of probable success, to be discussed under proportionality, is usually waived.

Offensive wars raise more complications. In classical just-war doctrine, offensive wars were permitted to protect vital rights unjustly threatened or injured. Moreover, in a form now archaic, offensive wars of vindictive justice against infidels and heretics were once permitted. Such wars disappeared with the decline of the religious, holy-war element as a cause of the rationale for wars. Thus, the forms of permissible wars today are twofold: wars of self-defense and offensive wars to enforce justice for oneself. As will be seen, even the second is now seemingly prohibited by positive international law. But in terms of basic just-war theory it remains an option. A war of vindictive justice wherein the belligerent fights against error and evil as a matter of principle and not of necessity is no longer condoned by just-war doctrine. . . .

Turning from the forms of just war we come to the heart of just cause—proportionality between the just ends and the means. This concerns the relationship between *raison d'état* (the high interests of state) and the use of the military instrument in war as the means to achieve these interests. This concept of proportionality at the level of *raison d'état* is multidimensional. To begin with, the ends held out as the just cause must be sufficiently good and important to warrant the extreme means of war, the arbitrament of arms. Beyond that, a projection of the outcome of the war is required in which the probable good expected to result from success is weighed against the probable evil that the war will cause.

The process of weighing probable good against probable evil is extremely complex. The balance sheet of good and evil must be estimated for each belligerent. Additionally, there should be a balancing of effects on individual third parties and on the international common good. International interdependence means that international conflicts are difficult to contain and that their shock waves affect third parties in a manner that must be accounted for in the calculus of probable good and evil. Moreover, the international community as such has its international common good, which is necessarily affected by any war. Manifestly, the task of performing this calculus effectively is an awesome one. But even its successful completion does not fully satisfy the demands of the just-war condition of just cause. Probing even further, the doctrine requires a responsible judgment that there is a probability of success for the just party. All of these calculations must be concluded convincingly to meet the multidimensional requirement of just cause.

Moreover, the calculus of proportionality between probable good and evil in a war is a continuing one. It should be made before the decision to go to war. It must then be reviewed at critical points along the process of waging the war. The best informed estimates about wars are often in error. They may need revision or replacement by completely new estimates. The *jus ad bellum* requirement of proportionality, then, includes these requirements:

There must be a just cause of sufficient importance to warrant its defense by recourse to armed coercion.

The probable good to be achieved by successful recourse to armed coercion in pursuit of the just cause must outweigh the probable evil that the war will produce.

The calculation of proportionality between probable good and evil must be made with respect to all belligerents, affected neutrals, and the international community as a whole before initiating a war and periodically throughout a war to reevaluate the balance of good and evil that is actually produced by war.

These calculations must be made in the light of realistic estimates of the probability of success. . . .

There is an important qualification to the requirement of probability of success. A war of self-defense may be engaged in irrespective of the prospects for success, particularly if there is a great threat to continued existence and to fundamental values. . . .

The last component of the condition of just cause is that war be employed only as a last resort after the exhaustion of peaceful alternatives. To have legitimate recourse to war, it must be the ultima ratio, the arbitrament of arms. This requirement has taken on added significance in the League of Nations–United Nations period. It was the intention of the nations that founded these international organizations to create the machinery for peace that would replace self-help in the form of recourse to war and limit the need for collective security enforcement action to extreme cases of defiance of international law and order. There are certainly adequate institutions of international negotiations, mediation, arbitration, and adjudication to accommodate any nation willing to submit its international disputes to peaceful settlement. Indeed, the existence of this machinery for peaceful settlement has prompted international lawyers and statesmen to adopt a rough rule of thumb: the state that fails to exhaust the peaceful remedies available before resorting to war is prima facie an aggressor. . . .

RIGHT INTENTION

Among the elements of the concept of right intention, several points may be distinguished. First, right intention limits the belligerent to the pursuit of the avowed just cause. That pursuit may not be turned into an excuse to pursue other causes that might not meet the conditions of just cause. Thus, if the just cause is to defend a nation's borders and protect them from future aggressions, but the fortunes of war place the just belligerent in the position to conquer the unjust nation, such a conquest might show a lack of right intention and change the just war into an unjust war. The just cause would have been realized by a war of limited objectives rather than a war of total conquest.

Second, right intention requires that the just belligerent have always in mind as the ultimate object of the war a just and lasting peace. There is an implicit requirement to prepare for reconciliation even as one wages war. This is a hard saying. It will often go against the grain of the belligerents' disposition, but pursuit of a just and lasting peace is an essential characteristic of the difference between just and unjust war. Accordingly, any belligerent acts that unnecessarily increase the destruction and bitterness of war and thereby endanger the prospects for true peace are liable to condemnation as violations of the condition of right intention.

Third, underlying the other requirements, right intention insists that charity and love exist even among enemies. Enemies must be treated as human beings with rights. The thrust of this requirement is twofold. Externally, belligerents must act with charity toward their enemies. Internally, belligerents must suppress natural animosity and hatred, which can be sinful and injurious to the moral and psychological health of those who fail in charity. Gratuitous cruelty may be harmful to those who indulge in it as to their victims.

Right intention raises difficult moral and psychological problems. It may well be that its tenets set standards that will often be unattainable insofar as the thoughts and feelings of belligerents are concerned. War often treats individuals and nations so cruelly and unfairly that it is unrealistic to expect them to banish all hatred of those who have afflicted them. We can, however, more reasonably insist that just belligerents may not translate their strong feelings into behavior that is prohibited by the rule of right intention. A nation may feel tempted to impose a Carthaginian peace, but it may not exceed just cause by giving in to that temptation. A nation must have good reason for feeling that the enemy deserves the full force of all means available, but the requirement to build for a just and lasting peace prohibits this kind of vengeance. The enemy may have behaved abominably, engendering righteous indignation amounting to hatred, but the actions of the just belligerent must be based on charity.

Lest this appear to be so utterly idealistic as to warrant dismissal as irrelevant to the real world, let it be recalled that the greatest enemies of the modern era have often been brought around in the cyclical processes of international policies to become trusted allies against former friends who are now viewed with fear and distrust. If war is to be an instrument of policy and not, in St. Augustine's words, a "vendetta," right intention is a counsel of good policy as well as of morality....

THE *JUS IN BELLO*

In the *jus in bello* that emerged rather late in the development of just-war doctrine, two basic limitations on the conduct of war were laid down. One was the principle of proportion requiring proportionality of military means to political and military ends. The other was the principle of discrimination prohibiting direct, intentional attacks on noncombatants and nonmilitary targets. These are the two categories of *jus in bello* limitations generally treated by modern workers on just war....

The Principle of Proportion

In the preceding [discussion] the principle of proportion was discussed at the level of *raison d'état*. One of the criteria of just-war *jus ad bellum* requires that the good to be achieved by the realization of the war aims be proportionate to the evil resulting from the war. When the principle of proportion is again raised in the *jus in bello,* the question immediately arises as to the referent of proportionality in judging the means of war. Are the means to be judged in relation to the end of the war, the ends being formulated in the highest *raison d'état* terms? Or are intermediate political/military goals, referred to in the law-of-war literature as *raison de guerre,* the more appropriate referents in the calculus of proportionality as regards the conduct of a war?

There is no question that the ultimate justification for all means in war lies in the just cause that is a political purpose, *raison d'état*. But there are difficulties in making the ends of *raison d'état* the sole referent in the *jus in bello* calculus of proportionality. First, relation of all means to the highest ends of the war gives little rationale for or justification of discrete military means. If all means are simply lumped together as allegedly necessary for the war effort, one has to accept or reject them wholly in terms of the just cause, leaving no morality of means. The calculus of proportionality in just cause is the total good to be expected if the war is successful balanced against the total evil the war is likely to cause.

Second, it is evident that a discrete military means could, when viewed independently on the basis of its intermediary military end (*raison de guerre*), be proportionate or disproportionate to that military end for which it was used, irrespective of the ultimate end of the war at the level of *raison d'état*. If such a discrete military means were proportionate in terms of its military end, it would be a legitimate belligerent act. If it were disproportionate to the military end, it would be immoral and legally impermissible. Thus, an act could be proportionate or disproportionate to a legitimate military end regardless of the legitimacy of the just-cause end of *raison d'état*.

Third, there is the need to be realistic and fair in evaluating individual command responsibility for belligerent acts. The need to distinguish higher political ends from intermediate military ends was acute in the war-crimes trial after World War II. It is the law of Nuremberg, generally accepted in international law, that the *raison d'état* ends of Nazi Germany were illegal aggression. But the Nuremberg and other war-crimes tribunals rejected the argument that all military actions taken by the German armed forces were war crimes per se because they were carried out in pursuance of aggressive war. The legitimacy of discrete acts of German forces was judged, inter alia, in terms of their proportionality to intermediate military goals, *raison de guerre*. This was a matter of justice to military commanders

accused of war crimes. It was also a reasonable way to evaluate the substance of the allegations that war crimes had occurred.

The distinction is equally important when applied to a just belligerent. Assuming that in World War II the Allied forces were fighting a just war, it is clear that some of the means they employed may have been unjust (for example, strategic bombing of cities and the two atomic bomb attacks). It is not difficult to assimilate these controversial means into the total Allied war effort and pronounce that total effort proportionate to the just cause of the war. It is much more difficult and quite a different calculation to justify these means as proportionate to discrete military ends. Even in the absence of war-crimes proceedings, a just belligerent ought to respect the *jus in bello* standards by meeting the requirement of proportionality of means to military ends.

To be sure, it is ultimately necessary to transcend concern for the responsibility of individual military commanders and look at the objective permissibility of a military means. Thus, it may be possible and necessary to absolve a commander from responsibility for an action taken that is judged to have been disproportionate but that appeared to him to be a proportionate, reasonable military action in the light of his imperfect estimate of the situation....

It would appear that analyses of the proportionality of military means will have to take a two-fold form. First, any military means must be proportionate to discrete, legitimate military end. Second, military means proportionate to discrete, legitimate military ends must also be proportionate to the object of the war, the just cause. In judging the moral and legal responsibility of a military commander, emphasis should be placed on the proportionality of the means to a legitimate military end. In judging the ultimate normative permissibility, as well as the prudential advisability, of a means at the level of *raison d'état*, the calculation should emphasize proportionality to the just cause.

The focus of normative analysis with respect to a means of war will depend on the place of the means in the total pattern of belligerent interaction. Means may be divided roughly according to the traditional distinction between tactical and strategic levels of war. Tactical means will normally be judged in terms of their proportionality to tactical military ends (for example, the tactics of attacking or defending a fortified population center will normally be judged in terms of their proportionality to the military end of taking or holding the center). Strategic means will normally be judged in terms of their proportionality to the political/military goals of the war (for example, the strategy of attacking Japanese cities, first conventionally and then with atomic bombs, in order to force the surrender of Japan will be judged in terms of its proportionality to the just cause of war).

It remains clear, however, that the two levels overlap. A number of tactical decisions regarding battles for population centers may produce an overall strategic pattern that ought to enter into the highest calculation of the proportionality of a just war. The strategic decisions, on the other hand, have necessary tactical implications (for example, strategic conventional and atomic bombing of Japan was an alternative to an amphibious invasion) the conduct of which is essentially a tactical matter. The potential costs of such a tactical invasion strongly influenced the strategic choice to seek Japan's defeat by strategic bombing rather than ground conquest.

Insofar as judgment of proportionality in terms of military ends is concerned, there is a central concept appearing in all normative analyses of human behavior—the norm of reasonableness. Reasonableness must always be defined in specific context. However, sometimes patterns of behavior recur so that there are typical situations for which common models of reasonable behavior may be prescribed. In domestic law this norm is concretized through the device of the hypothetically reasonable man whose conduct sets the standard to be emulated by law-abiding persons. The reasonable commander is the counterpart of the reasonable man in the law of war. The construct of the reasonable commander is based upon the experience of military men in dealing with basic military problems.

Formulation of this experience into the kinds of working guidelines that domestic law provides, notable in the field of torts, has not advanced very far....We do, however, have some instances in which this approach was followed. For example, the U.S. military tribunal in the *Hostage* case found that certain retaliatory means used in the German military in occupied Europe in World War II were reasonable in view of the threat to the belligerent occupant posed by guerrilla operations and their support by the civilian population. On the other hand, in the *Calley* case a court comprised of experienced combat officers found that Lieutenant Calley's response to the situation in My Lai was altogether unreasonable, below the standard of reasonableness expected in combat in Vietnam.

The difficulty with establishing the standards of reasonableness lies in the absence of authoritative decisions that can be widely disseminated for mandatory emulation. In a domestic public order such as the United States, the legislature and the courts set standards for reasonable behavior. While the standards have supporting rationales, their greater strength lies in the fact that they are laid down by authority and must be obeyed. With the very rare exception of some of the post–World War II war-crimes cases, authoritative standards for belligerent conduct are found primarily in general conventional and customary international-law prescriptions....

The Principle of Discrimination

The principle of discrimination prohibits direct intentional attacks on noncombatants and non-military targets. It holds out the potential for very great, specific limitations on the conduct of just war. Accordingly, debates over the meaning of the *principle of discrimination* have become increasingly complex and important as the character of war has become more total. It is in the nature of the principle of proportion to be elastic and to offer possibilities for justifications of means that are truly necessary for efficacious military action. However, it is in the nature of the principle of discrimination to remain rigidly opposed to various categories of means irrespective of their necessity to success in war. It is not surprising, then, that most debates about the morality of modern war have focused on the principle of discrimination.

Such debates are vastly complicated by the opportunities afforded in the defiance of the principle of discrimination to expand or contract it by interpretations of its component elements. There are debates over the meaning of *direct intentional attack, noncombatants,* and *military targets.*

In order to discuss the problem of interpreting the principle of discrimination, it is necessary to understand the origins of the principle. The most fundamental aspect of the principle of discrimination lies in its direct relation to the justification for killing in war. If the presumption against killing generally and war in particular is overcome (in the case of war by meeting the just-war conditions), the killing then permitted is limited to the enemy combatants, the aggressors. The exceptional right to take life in individual self-defense and in war is limited to the attacker in the individual case and the enemy's soldiers in the case of war. One may not attack innocent third parties as part of individual self-defense. In war the only permissible objects of direct attack are the enemy's soldiers. In both cases, the overriding moral prescription is that evil must not be done to obtain a good object. As will be seen, however, the literal application of the principle of discrimination tends to conflict with the characteristics of efficacious military action necessary to make the right of just war effective and meaningful.

However, it is important to recognize that the principle of discrimination did not find its historical origins solely or even primarily in the fundamental argument summarized above. As a matter of fact, the principle seems to have owed at least as much to codes of chivalry and to the subsequent development of positive customary laws of war. These chivalric codes and customary practices were grounded in the material characteristics of warfare during the medieval and Renaissance periods. During much of that time, the key to the conduct of war was combat between mounted knights and supporting infantry. Generally speaking, there was no military utility in attacking anyone other than the enemy knights and their armed retainers. Attacks on unarmed civilians, particularly women and children, would have been considered unchivalric, contrary to the customary law of war, and militarily gratuitous.

These multiple bases for noncombatant immunity were fortified by the growth of positive international law after the seventeenth century. In what came to be known as the Rousseau-Portalis Doctrine, war was conceived as being limited to what we could call today "counterforce warfare." Armies fought each other like athletic teams designated to represent national banners. The noncombatants were spectators to these struggles and, unless they had the bad fortune to find themselves directly on the battlefield, immune in principle from military attack. Attacks on noncombatants and nonmilitary targets were now prohibited by a rule of positive international law. Here again, the principle of discrimination was grounded in material facts, the state of the art and the limited nature of the conflicts, that continued to make possible its application. Moreover, the political philosophy of the time encouraged a separation of public armed forces and the populations they represented. All of these military and political supports for discrimination were to change with the advent of modern war.

At this point it is necessary to clarify the status of the principle of discrimination in just-war doctrine as interpreted in this chapter. It is often contended that there is an absolute principle of discrimination prohibiting any use of means that kill noncombatants. It is further contended that this absolute principle constitutes the central limitation of just war and that it is based on an immutable moral imperative that may never be broken no matter how just the cause. This is the moral axiom mentioned above, that evil may never be done in order to produce a good result. In this formulation, killing noncombatants intentionally is always an inadmissible evil.

These contentions have produced two principal reactions. The first is pacifism. Pacifists rightly argue that war inevitably involves violation of the absolute principle of discrimination. If that principle is unconditionally binding, a just war is difficult if not impossible to envisage. The second reaction to the claims of an absolute principle of discrimination is to modify the principle by some form of the principle of double effect whereby the counterforce component of a military means is held to represent the intent of the belligerent, whereas the countervalue, indiscriminate component of that means is explained as a tolerable, concomitant, unintended effect—collateral damage in contemporary strategic terms.

Paul Ramsey is unquestionably the most authoritative proponent of an absolute principle of discrimination as the cornerstone of just-war *jus in bello*. No one has tried more courageously to reconcile this absolute principle with the exigencies of modern war and deterrence. [But] neither Ramsey nor anyone else can reconcile the principle of discrimination in an absolute sense with the strategic countervalue nuclear warfare that is threatened in contemporary deterrence. It is possible that Ramsey's version of discrimination could survive the pressures of military necessity at levels below that of strategic nuclear deterrence and war. But the fate of Ramsey's effort to reconcile an absolute moral principle of discrimination with the characteristics of modern war should indicate the grave difficulties inherent in this effort. . . .

The question then arises whether such heroic efforts to salvage an absolute principle of discrimination are necessary. As observed above, the principle of discrimination does not appear in the just-war *jus in bello* as a doctrinally established deduction from theological or philosophical first principles. Rather, it was historically the product of belligerent practice reflecting a mixture of moral and cultural values of earlier societies. Moreover, it is significant that in the considerable body of contemporary Catholic social teaching on war, embracing the pronouncements of Pope Pius XII and his successors and of Vatican II, the principle of discrimination is not prominent in any form, absolute or conditional. When weapons systems or forms of warfare are condemned, deplored, or reluctantly condoned, the rationales are so generalized that the judgments appear to be based on a mixed application of the principles of proportion and discrimination. If anything, these pronouncements seem more concerned with disproportionate rather than indiscriminate effects.

It is a curious kind of supreme, absolute principle of the just-war doctrine that slips almost imperceptibly into the evolving formulations of the authoritative texts and then is omitted as an explicit controlling rationale in contemporary judgments by the church framed in just-war terms. Moreover, the persistent reiteration by the contemporary church that legitimate self-defense is still morally permissible should imply that such defense is practically feasible; otherwise the recognition of the right is meaningless. But, as the pacifists rightly observe, self-defense or any kind of war is incompatible with an absolute principle of discrimination.

It is my contention that the moral, just-war principle of discrimination is not an absolute limitation on belligerent conduct. There is no evidence that such a principle was ever seriously advanced by the church, and it is implicitly rejected when the church acknowledges the continued right of legitimate self-defense, a right that has always been incompatible with observance of an absolute principle of discrimination. Accordingly, I do not distinguish an absolute, moral, just-war principle of discrimination from a more flexible and variable international-law principle of discrimination. To be sure, the moral, just-war understanding of discrimination must remain independent of that of international law at any given time. But discrimination is best understood and most effectively applied in light of the interpretations of the principle in the practice of belligerents. This, after all, was the principal origin of this part of the *jus in bello,* and the need to check moral just-war formulations against contemporary international-law versions is perennial.

Such a position is in no sense a retreat from a position of maximizing normative limitations on the conduct of war. In the first place, as Ramsey's brave but ultimately unsuccessful efforts have demonstrated, attachment to an absolute principle of discrimination leads either to a finding that all war is immoral and the demise of the just-war doctrine or to tortured efforts to reconcile the irreconcilable. Neither serves the purposes of the *jus in bello*. Second, the rejection of an absolute principle of discrimination does not mean an abandonment of efforts to limit war on moral grounds. The principle of discrimination remains a critical source of both moral and legal limitations of belligerent behavior. As Tucker has observed, there are significant points of limitation between the position that no injury must ever be done to noncombatants and the position that there are no restraints on countervalue warfare. The interpretations that follow here . . . will try to balance the need to protect noncombatants with the need to recognize the legitimate military necessities of modern forms of warfare. In this process one may err one way or the other, but at least some relevant, practical guidance may be offered belligerents. Adherence to an absolute principle of discrimination usually means irrelevance to the question of limiting the means of war or unconvincing casuistry.

In search of such practical guidance one may resume the examination of the principle of discrimination as interpreted both by moralists and international lawyers. Even before the principle of discrimination was challenged by the changing realities of total war, there were practical difficulties with the definition of *direct international attack, noncombatants,* and *nonmilitary targets.* It is useful, as a starting point for analysis, to recall a standard and authoritative exposition of the principle of discrimination by Fr. Richard McCormick.

> It is a fundamental moral principle [unanimously accepted by Catholic moralists] that it is immoral directly to take innocent human life except with divine authorization. "Direct" taking of human life implies that one performs a lethal action with the intention that death should result for himself or another. Death therefore is deliberately willed as the effect of one's action. "Indirect" killing refers to an action or omission that is designed and intended solely to achieve some other purpose(s) even though death is foreseen as a concomitant effect. Death therefore is not positively willed, but is reluctantly permitted as an unavoidable by-product.[2]

As example that is frequently used in connection with this question is the use of catapults in medieval sieges of castles. The intention—indeed, the purpose—of catapulting projectiles over the castle wall was to kill enemy defenders and perhaps to break down the defenses. If noncombatants—innocents as they were called then—were killed or injured, this constituted a "concomitant effect," an "undesired by-product."

The issues of intention, act, and multiple effects are often analyzed in terms of the principle of double effect, which Father McCormick's exposition employs without invoking the concept explicitly. After centuries of inconclusive efforts to apply the principle of double effect to the *jus in bello,* Michael Walzer has proposed his own version, which merits reflection and experimental application.

> The intention of the actor is good, that is, he aims narrowly at the acceptable effect; the evil effect is not one of his ends, nor is it a means to his ends, and, aware of the evil involved, he seeks to minimize it, accepting costs to himself.[3]

It is probably not possible to reconcile observance of the principle of discrimination with the exigencies of genuine military necessity without employing the principle of double effect in one form or another. However this distinction between primary, desired effect and secondary, concomitant, undesired by-product is often difficult to accept.

It is not so hard to accept the distinction in a case where the concomitant undesired effect was accidental (for example, a case where the attacker did not know that noncombatants were present in the target area). There would still remain in such a case a question as to whether the attacker ought to have known that noncombatants might be present. Nor is it so hard to accept a double-effect justification in a situation where the attacker had reason to believe that there might be noncombatants present but that this was a remote possibility. If, however, the attacker knows that

---

[2]"Morality of War," *New Catholic Encyclopedia* 14 (1967), p. 805.

[3]Michael Walzer, *Just and Unjust Wars* (New York: Basic Books, 1977), p. 155.

there are noncombatants intermingled with combatants to the point that any attack on the military target is highly likely to kill or injure noncombatants, then the death or injury to those noncombatants is certainly "intended" or "deliberately willed," in the common usage of those words.

Turning to the object of the protection of the principle of discrimination—the innocents or noncombatants—another critical question of interpretation arises. How does one define noncombatants? How does one define nonmilitary targets? The assumption of separability of military forces and the populations they represented, found in medieval theory and continued by the Rousseau-Portalis Doctrine, became increasingly less valid after the wars of the French Revolution.

As nations engaged in total mobilization, one society or system against another, it was no longer possible to distinguish sharply between the military forces and the home fronts that rightly held themselves out as critical to the war effort. By the American Civil War this modern phenomenon had assumed critical importance. The material means of supporting the Confederate war effort were attacked directly and intentionally by Union forces. War in the age of the Industrial Revolution was waged against the sources of war production. Moreover, the nature of the attacks on noncombatants was psychological as well as material. Military forces have always attempted to break the will of the opposing forces as well as to destroy or scatter them. It now became the avowed purpose of military forces to break the will of the home front as well as to destroy its resources for supporting the war. This, of course, was to become a major purpose of modern strategic aerial bombardment.

To be sure, attacks on the bases of military forces have historically often been an effective strategy. But in the simpler world before the Industrial Revolution, this was not such a prominent option. When the huge conscript armies began to fight for profound ideological causes with the means provided by modern industrial mobilization and technology, the home front and consequently the noncombatants became a critical target for direct intentional attack.

The question then arose whether a civilian could be a participant in the overall was effort to such a degree as to lose his previous noncombatant immunity. Likewise, it became harder to distinguish targets that were clearly military from targets, such as factories or railroad facilities, that were of sufficient military importance to justify their direct intentional attack. It is important to note that this issue arose before the great increase in the range, areas of impact, and destructive effects of modern weaponry, conventional and nuclear. What we may term *countervalue warfare* was carried out in the American Civil War not because it was dictated by the weapons systems but because the civilian population and war-related industries and activities were considered to be critical and legitimate targets to be attacked.

In World War I this kind of attack was carried out primarily by the belligerents with their maritime blockades. Above all, these blockades caused the apparent demise of the principle of noncombatant immunity in the positive international law of war. Other factors in this demise were developments that revealed potentials not fully realized until World War II (for example, aerial bombardment of population centers and unrestricted submarine warfare). In World War II aerial bombardment of population centers was preeminent as a source of attacks on traditional noncombatants and nonmilitary targets. By this time the concept of total mobilization had advanced so far that a plausible argument could be made that vast segments of belligerent populations and complexes of industry and housing had become so integral to the war effort as to lose their noncombatant immunity.

In summary, well before the advent of weapons systems that are usually employed in ways that do not discriminate between traditional combatants and noncombatants, military and nonmilitary targets, the distinction had eroded. The wall of separation between combatants and noncombatants had been broken down by the practice of total societal mobilization in modern total war and the resulting practice of attacking directly and intentionally that mobilization base. Given these developments, it was difficult to maintain that the principle of discrimination was still a meaningful limit on war. Those who clung to the principle tended to reject modern war altogether as inherently immoral because it inherently violates the principle. In the international law of war, distinguished publicists were reduced to stating that terror bombing of noncombatants with no conceivable proximate military utility was prohibited, but that the rights of noncombatants to protection otherwise were unclear....

✂ REVIEW QUESTIONS

1. O'Brien states three conditions for permissible recourse to war. What are they?
2. What problems arise in trying to satisfy the first condition?
3. How does O'Brien explain the four subdivisions of the just cause condition?
4. What are the elements of the concept of right intention according to O'Brien?
5. Explain the principles of proportion and discrimination as O'Brien applies them to the conduct in war.

✂ DISCUSSION QUESTIONS

1. O'Brien says that offensive war remains an option in just war theory. When, if ever, would an offensive war be justified?
2. According to O'Brien, right intention insists that charity and love exist even among enemies. Are charity and love compatible with killing and injuring people?
3. O'Brien thinks that the bombing of Hiroshima and Nagasaki was allowed by just war theory. Do you agree? Didn't this killing of 200,000 innocent people violate the principle of discrimination?

The Terrorist's Tacit Message*

LAURIE CALHOUN

Laurie Calhoun is the author of *Philosophy Unmasked: A Skeptic's Critique* (1997) and many essays on ethics, rhetoric, and war.

Calhoun applies just war theory to terrorism. Terrorism is condemned by the governments of democratic nations, who continue to engage in "just wars." But when the assumptions involved in the "just war" approach to group conflict are examined, it emerges that terrorists merely follow these assumptions to their logical conclusion. They see themselves fighting "just wars," as "warriors for justice." That is their tacit message. Accordingly, unless the stance toward war embraced by most governments of the world transforms radically, terrorism can be expected to continue over time. As groups proliferate, so will conflicts, and some groups will resort to deadly force, reasoning along "just war" lines. Because terrorists are innovative strategists, it is doubtful that measures based upon conventional military operations will effectively counter terrorism.

Source: Reprinted from *The Peace Review*, Vol. 14, No. 1 (2002). Reprinted with permission from Taylor & Francis Ltd.
*Editor's Note: This article was written before 9/11.

The refusal to "negotiate with terrorists" is a common refrain in political parlance. It is often accepted as self-evident that terrorists are so far beyond the pale that it would be morally reprehensible even to engage in discourse with them. But the term "terrorist" remains elusive, defined in various ways by various parties, albeit always derogatorily. Judging from the use of the term by the government officials of disparate nations, it would seem to be analytically true that, whoever the speakers may be, they are not terrorists. "Terrorists" refers exclusively to *them*, a lesser or greater set of political actors, depending ultimately upon the sympathies of the speaker.

Government leaders often speak as though terrorists are beyond the reach of reason, but particular terrorists in particular places believe that they are transmitting to the populace a message with concrete content. The message invariably takes the following general form: *There is something seriously wrong with the world in which we live, and this must be changed.* Terrorists sometimes claim to have as their aim to rouse the populace to consciousness so that they might at last see what the terrorists take themselves to have seen. However, the members of various terrorist groups together transmit (unwittingly) a more global message. The lesson that we ought to glean from terrorists is not the specific, context-dependent message that they hope through their use of violence to convey. Terrorists are right that there is something seriously wrong with the world in which we and they live, but they are no less a party to the problem than are the governments against which they inveigh.

That the annihilation of human life is sometimes morally permissible or even obligatory is embodied in two social practices: the execution of criminals and the maintenance of military institutions. This suggests that there are two distinct ways of understanding terrorists' interpretations of their own actions. Either they are attempting to effect "vigilante justice," or else they are fighting "just wars." Because their victims are typically non-combatants, terrorist actions more closely resemble acts of war than vigilante killings. There are of course killers who do not conceive of their own crimes along these lines, having

themselves no political agenda or moral mission. Unfortunately, the tendency of governments to conflate terrorists with ordinary murderers (without political agendas) shrouds the similarity between the violent activities of factional groups and those of formal nations.

Attempts to identify "terrorists" by appeal to what these people do give rise to what some might find to be embarrassing implications. For example, to specify "terrorism" as necessarily *illegal* leads to problems in interpreting the reign of terror imposed by the Third Reich in Nazi Germany and other governmental regimes of ill repute. One might, then, propose a moral rather than a legal basis, for example, by delineating "terrorists" as *ideologically or politically motivated actors who kill or threaten to kill innocent people bearing no responsibility for the grievances of the killers.* This would imply that every nation that has engaged in bombing campaigns resulting in the deaths of innocent children has committed acts of terrorism. Faced with this proposed assimilation of nations and factions that deploy deadly force, most people will simply back away, insisting that, though a precise definition is not possible, certain obvious examples of terrorists can be enumerated, and so "terrorist" can be defined by ostension.

The governments of democratic nations harshly condemn "terrorists," but when the assumptions involved in any view according to which war is sometimes just are carefully examined, it emerges that terrorists merely follow these assumptions to their logical conclusion, given the situations in which they find themselves. While nations prohibit the use of deadly force by individuals and sub-national factions, in fact, violent attacks upon strategic targets can be understood straightforwardly as permitted by "just war" rationales, at least as interpreted by the killers. Small terrorist groups could not, with any chance of success, attack a formal military institution, so instead they select targets for their shock appeal.

While secrecy is often thought to be of the very essence of terrorism, the covert practices of terrorist groups are due in part to their illegality. The members of such groups often hide their identities (or at least their own involvement in particular acts of terrorism), not because they believe that their actions are wrong, but because it would be imprudent to expose themselves. Clearly, if one is subject to arrest for publicly committing an act, then one's efficacy as a soldier for the cause in question will be short-lived. Committing illegal acts in the open renders an actor immediately vulnerable to arrest and incarceration, but it is precisely because factional groups reject the legitimacy of the reigning regime that they undertake secretive initiatives best understood as militarily strategic. "Intelligence agencies" are an important part of modern military institutions, and secrecy has long been regarded as integral to martial excellence. Sun Tzu, author of the ancient Chinese classic *The Art of War,* observed nearly three thousand years ago that "All warfare is based on deception."

It is perhaps often simply terrorists' fervent commitment to their cause that leads them to maximize the efficacy of their campaigns by sheltering themselves from vulnerability to the laws of the land, as any prudent transgressor of the law would do. At the other extreme, suicide missions, in which agents openly act in ways that lead to their personal demise, are undertaken only when such martyrdom appears to be the most effective means of drawing attention to the cause. Far from being beyond rational comprehension, the actions of terrorists are dictated by military strategy deployed in the name of what the actors believe to be justice. The extreme lengths to which terrorists are willing to go, the sacrifices that they will make in their efforts to effect a change in the *status quo,* evidence their ardent commitment to their cause.

The common construal of war as a sometimes "necessary evil" implies that war may be waged when the alternative (not waging war) would be worse. If the military could have achieved its objectives without killing innocent people, then it would have done so. Military spokesmen have often maintained that unintended civilian deaths, even when foreseen, are permissible, provided the situation is sufficiently grave. In the just war tradition, what matters, morally speaking, is

whether such "collateral damage" is intended by the actors. Equally integral to defenses of the moral permissibility of collateral damage is the principle of last resort, according to which non-belligerent means must have been attempted and failed. If war is not a last resort, then collateral damage is avoidable and therefore morally impermissible. Few would deny that, if there exist ways to resolve a conflict without destroying innocent persons in the process, then those methods must, morally speaking, be pursued. But disputes arise, in specific contexts, regarding whether in fact non-belligerent means to conflict resolution exist. To say that during wartime people *resort* to deadly force is to say that they have a reason, for it is of the very nature of justification to advert to reasons. Defenders of the recourse by nations to deadly force as a means of conflict resolution are willing to condone the killing of innocent people under certain circumstances. The question becomes: When have non-belligerent means been exhausted?

Perhaps the most important (though seldom acknowledged) problem with just war theory is its inextricable dependence upon the interpretation of the very people considering recourse to deadly force. Human fallibility is a given, so in owning that war is justified in some cases, one must acknowledge that the "facts" upon which a given interpretation is based may prove to be false. And anyone who affirms the right (or obligation) to wage war when *they believe* the tenets of just war theory to be satisfied, must, in consistency, also affirm this right (or obligation) for all those who find themselves in analogous situations. But throughout human history wars have been characterized by their instigators as "just," including those retrospectively denounced as grossly unjust, for example, Hitler's campaign. People tend to ascribe good intentions to their own leaders and comrades while ascribing evil intentions to those stigmatized by officials as "the enemy."

The simplicity of its intuitive principles accounts for the widespread appeal of the "just war" paradigm. Throughout human history appeals to principles of "just cause" and "last resort" have been made by both sides to virtually every violent conflict. "Just war" rationalizations are available to everyone, Hussein as well as Bush, Milosevic as well as Clinton. To take a recent example, we find Timothy McVeigh characterizing the deaths of innocent people in the Oklahoma City bombing as "collateral damage." The public response to McVeigh's "preposterous" appropriation of just war theory suggests how difficult it is for military supporters to admit that they are not so very different from the political killers whose actions they condemn.

The received view is that the intention of planting bombs in public places such as the Federal Building in Oklahoma City or the World Trade Center in New York City is to terrorize, and the people who do such things are terrorists. According to the received view, though some innocent people may have been traumatized and killed during the Vietnam War, the Gulf War, and NATO's 1999 bombing campaign in Kosovo, whatever the intentions behind those actions may have been, they certainly were not to *terrorize* people. Nations excuse as regrettable, though unavoidable the deaths of children such as occurred during the Gulf War, the Vietnam War, and in Kosovo during NATO's bombing campaign against the regime of Slobodan Milosevic. "Terrorists" are the people who threaten or deploy deadly force for causes of which we do not approve.

Political organizations have often engaged in actions intended to instill fear in the populace and thus draw attention to their cause. But the groups that engage in what is typically labeled "terrorism" are motivated by grievances no less than are nations engaged in war. Were their grievances somehow alleviated, dissenting political groups would no longer feel the need to engage in what they interpret to be "just wars." In appropriating military rationales and tactics, terrorists underscore the obvious, that nations are conventionally assembled groups of people who appoint their leaders just as do sub-national factions. The problem with the received view is that it exercises maximal interpretive charity when it comes to nations (most often, the interpreter's own), while minimal interpretive charity when it comes to sub-national groups. The intention of a terrorist act, *as understood by the terrorist*, is not the immediate act of terrorism, but to air some grave concern, which the terrorist is attempting to bring to the public's attention. In reality, the requirement of "last resort" seems far simpler to fulfill in the cases of smaller, informal factional groups than in those involving a first-world super power such as the United States, the economic policies of which can, with only minor modifications, spell catastrophe for an offending regime. According to the just war tradition, the permissible use of deadly force is a last resort, deployed only after all pacific means have proven infeasible, and the terrorist most likely reasons along precisely these lines. Indeed, the urgency of the terrorist's situation (to his own mind) makes his own claims regarding last resort all the more compelling. A terrorist, no less than the military spokesmen of established nations, may regret the deaths of the innocent people to which his activities give rise. But, applying the "just war" approach to "collateral damage," terrorists may emerge beyond moral reproach, since were their claims adequately addressed by the powers that be, they would presumably cease their violent activities. It is because they believe that their rights have been denied that groups engage in the activities identified as "terrorism" and thought by most people to be morally distinct from the military actions of states.

Once one grants the possibility of a "just war," it seems to follow straightforwardly that political dissidents convinced of the unjust practices of the government in power ought to engage in violent acts of subversion. Factions lack the advantage of currently enshrined institutions that naturally perpetuate the very *status quo* claimed by dissidents to be unjust. Accordingly, so long as nations continue to wage wars in the name of "justice," it seems plausible that smaller groups and factions will do so as well. Many terrorist groups insist that their claims have been squelched or ignored by the regime in power. But if formal nations may wage war to defend their own integrity and sovereignty, then why not separatist groups? And if such a group lacks a nationally funded and sanctioned army, then must not the group assemble its own?

The terrorist is not a peculiar type of creature who nefariously resorts to deadly force in opposition to the demands of morality upheld by all civilized nations. Rather, the terrorist merely embraces the widely held view that deadly military action is morally permissible, while delimiting "nations" differently than do those who uncritically accept the conventions which they have been raised to believe. The nations in existence are historically contingent, not a part of the very essence of things. The terrorist recognizes that current nations came into being and transformed as a result of warfare. Accordingly, agents who, in the name of justice, wield deadly force against the society in which they live conceive of themselves as civil warriors. Terrorist groups are smaller armies than those of established nations funded by taxpayers and sanctioned by the law, but for this very reason they may feel compelled to avail themselves of particularly drastic methods. No less than the military leaders of most countries throughout history, terrorists maintain that the situations which call for war are so desperate as to require the extremest of measures.

That a terrorist is not *sui generis* can be illustrated as follows: Imagine the commander-in-chief of any established nation being, instead, the leader of a group dissenting from the currently reigning regime. The very same person's acts of deadly violence (or his ordering his comrades to commit such acts) do not differ in his own mind merely because he has been formally designated the commander-in-chief in one case but not in the other. Both parties to every conflict maintain that they are right and their adversaries wrong, and terrorist factions are not exceptional in this respect. When we look carefully at the situation of terrorists, it becomes difficult to identify any morally significant distinction between what they do and what formal nations do in flying planes over enemy nations and dropping bombs, knowing full well that innocent people will die as a result of their actions.

Most advanced nations with standing armies not only produce but also export the types of deadly weapons used by factions in terrorist actions. If we restrict the use of the term "terrorist" to those groups that deploy deadly violence "beyond the pale" of any established legal system, then it follows that terrorists derive their weapons from more formal (and legal) military institutions and industries. The conventional weapons trade has proven all but impossible to control, given the ease with which stockpiled arms are transferred from regime to regime and provided by some countries to smaller groups that they deem to be politically correct. And even when scandals such as Iran-Contra are brought to light, seldom are the culpable agents held more than nominally accountable for their actions. Leniency toward military personnel and political leaders who engage in or facilitate patriotic though illegal weapons commerce results from the basic assumption on the part of most people, that they and their comrades are good, while those who disagree are not.

In some cases, terrorists develop innovative weapons through the use of materials with non-military applications, for example, sulfuric acid or ammonium nitrate. Given the possibility for innovative destruction by terrorist groups, it would seem that even more instrumental to the perpetuation of terrorism than the ongoing exportation of deadly weapons is the support by national leaders of *the idea* that killing human beings can be a mandate of justice. Bombing campaigns serve as graphic illustrations of the approbation by governments of the use of deadly force. It is simple indeed to understand what must be a common refrain among members of dissenting groups who adopt violent means: "If they can do it, then why cannot we?"

Political groups have agendas, and some of these groups deploy violence strategically in attempting to effect their aims. Terrorists are not "beyond the pale," intellectually and morally speaking, for their actions are best understood through appeal to the very just war theory invoked by nations in defending their own military campaigns. Terrorists interpret their own wars as just, while holding culpable all those who benefit from the policies of the government with which they disagree. The groups commonly identified as "terrorists" disagree with governments about not whether there can be a just war, nor whether morality is of such paramount importance as sometimes to require the killing of innocent people. Terrorist groups and the military institutions of nations embrace the very same "just war" schema, disagreeing only about facts.

Thus we find that the terrorist conveys two distinct messages. First, and this is usually the only claim to truth recognized by outsiders, the terrorist alleges injustices within the framework of society. In many cases there may be some truth to the specific charges made by terrorist groups, and this would be enough to turn against them all those who benefit from the regime in power. But a second and more important type of truth is highlighted by the very conduct of the terrorist. Perhaps there is something profoundly misguided about not only some of the specific policies within our societies, but also the manner in which we conceptualize the institutionalized use of deadly force, the activity of war, as an acceptable route to dispute resolution.

The connotations associated with "terrorist" are strongly pejorative and, although terrorists clearly operate from within what they take to be a moral framework, they are often subject to much more powerful condemnation than nonpolitical killers. But murderers who reject the very idea of morality would seem to be worse enemies of society than are political terrorists, who are motivated primarily by moral considerations. Why is it, then, that people fear and loathe terrorists so intensely? Perhaps they recognize, on some level, that terrorists are operating along lines that society in fact implicitly condones and even encourages. Perhaps people see shadows of themselves and their own activities in those of terrorists.

If it is true that terrorists view themselves as warriors for justice, then unless the stance toward war embraced by most governments of the world transforms radically, terrorism should be expected to continue over time. To the extent to which groups proliferate, conflicts will as well, and some subset of the parties to conflict will resort to deadly force, buoyed by what they, along with most of the populace, take to be the respectability of "just war." Military solutions are no longer used even by stable nations merely as "last resorts." Tragically, the ready availability of deadly weapons and the widespread assumption that the use of such weapons is often morally acceptable, if not obligatory, has brought about a world in which leaders often think first, not last, of military solutions to conflict. This readiness to deploy deadly means has arguably contributed to the escalation of violence in the contemporary world on many different levels, the most frightening of which being to many people those involving the unpredictable actions of factional groups, "the terrorists." But the leaders of established nations delude themselves in thinking that they will quell terrorism through threats and weapons proliferation. Terrorists "innovate" by re-defining what are commonly thought of as non-military targets as military. There is no reason for believing that terrorists' capacity for innovation will be frustrated by the construction of an anti-ballistic missile system or the implementation of other initiatives premised upon conventional military practices and strategies.

⅍ RECOMMENDED READINGS

Arendt, Hannah. 1979. *The Origins of Totalitarianism.* New York: Harcourt Brace.

Calhoun, Laurie. 2002. "How Violence Breeds Violence: Some Utilitarian Considerations," *Politics,* vol. 22, no. 2, pp. 95–108.

Calhoun, Laurie. 2001. "Killing, Letting Die, and the Alleged Necessity of Military Intervention," *Peace and Conflict Studies,* vol. 8, no. 2, pp. 5–22.

Calhoun, Laurie. 2001. "The Metaethical Paradox of Just War Theory," *Ethical Theory and Moral Practice,* vol. 4, no. 1, pp. 41–58.

Calhoun, Laurie. 2002. "The Phenomenology of Paid Killing," *International Journal of Human Rights,* vol. 6, no. 1, pp. 1–18.

Calhoun, Laurie. 2001. "Violence and Hypocrisy," and "Laurie Calhoun replies [to Michael Walzer]," *Dissent,* (winter) vol. 48, no. 1, pp. 79–87. Reprinted in *Just War: A Casebook in Argumentation,* eds. Walsh & Asch, Heinle/ Thomson, 2004.

Cerovic, Stanko. 2001. *Dans les griffes des humanistes,* trans. Mireille Robin. Paris: Éditions Climats.

Colson, Bruno. 1999. *L'art de la guerre de Machiavel à Clausewitz*. Namur: Bibliothèque Universitaire Moretus Plantin.

Cooper, H. H. A. 2001. "Terrorism: The Problem of Definition Revisited," *American Behavioral Scientist*, vol. 44, no. 6, pp. 881–893.

Gibbs, Jack P. 1989. "Conceptualization of Terrorism," *American Sociological Review*, vol. 54, no. 3, pp. 329–340.

Grossman, Lt. Colonel Dave. 1995. *On Killing: The Psychological Cost of Learning to Kill in War and Society*. Boston: Little Brown.

Harman, Gilbert. 2000. *Explaining Value*. Oxford: Oxford University Press.

Harman, Gilbert. 1977. *The Nature of Morality*. New York: Oxford University Press.

Holmes, Robert L. 1989. *On War and Morality*. Princeton: Princeton University Press.

Le Borgne, Claude. 1986. *La Guerre est Morte . . . mais on ne le sait pas encore*. Paris: Bernard Grasset.

Rapoport, David C. 1984. "Fear and Trembling: Terrorism in Three Religious Traditions," *The American Political Science Review*, vol. 78, no. 3, pp. 658–677.

✎ REVIEW QUESTIONS

1. According to Calhoun, what is the concrete message of terrorists? What is the more global message, the "tacit message"?
2. What problems does Calhoun see with the legal and moral definitions of "terrorists"?
3. How do terrorists view their actions according to Calhoun?
4. How do military spokesmen justify "collateral damage," or the killing of innocent people, according to Calhoun?
5. What role does interpretation play in just war theory, in Calhoun's view? Why does she think that "just war" rationalizations are available to everyone, from Hussein to Bush?
6. According to Calhoun, what is the intention of the terrorist act, as understood by the terrorist?
7. Why does Calhoun believe that terrorism is best understood by appealing to the very just war theory invoked by nations defending their wars?

✎ DISCUSSION QUESTIONS

1. Calhoun argues that anyone can rationalize war or terrorism by appealing to just war theory. Is this true or not? Why or why not?
2. Calhoun says, "Terrorists are people who threaten or deploy deadly force for causes of which we do not approve." Do you agree? Why or why not?
3. Calhoun claims that there is hardly any moral difference between what the terrorists do and what nations such as the United States do when they drop bombs on enemy nations knowing full well that innocent people will die. Do you agree? Why or why not?

What Is Terrorism?

LOUISE RICHARDSON

Louise Richardson is executive dean of the Radcliffe Institute for Advanced Study, a senior lecturer in government at Harvard, and a lecturer on law at Harvard Law School. She is the author of *What Terrorists Want* (2006), from which our reading is taken, and *When Allies*

Source: "What Is Terrorism?" by Louise Richardson from *What Terrorists Want*, pp. 4–6, 14–20. NY: Random House, 2006.

Differ (1996). She is the editor of *The Roots of Terrorism* (2006) and a coeditor of *Democracy and Counterterrorism* (2006). She has published numerous articles and book chapters on the subject of terrorism.

Richardson defines terrorism as deliberately and violently targeting civilians for political purposes. The point is to send a message. To do this, the act and the victim usually have symbolic significance. The audience for the message is not the same as the victim of the violence. On her view, terrorism is not the act of a state but of substate terrorist groups. She argues that terrorists are not insane, and they can and do use various defenses to justify their actions.

Terrorism simply means deliberately and violently targeting civilians for political purposes. It has seven crucial characteristics. First, a terrorist act is politically inspired. If not, then it is simply a crime. After the May 13, 2003, Riyadh bombings, Secretary of State Colin Powell declared, "We should not try to cloak their...criminal activity, their murderous activity, in any trappings of political purpose. They are terrorists." In point of fact, it is precisely because they did have a political purpose that they were, indeed, terrorists.

Second, if an act does not involve violence or the threat of violence, it is not terrorism. The term "cyberterrorism" is not a useful one. The English lexicon is broad enough to provide a term for the sabotage of our IT facilities without reverting to such language.

Third, the point of terrorism is not to defeat the enemy but to send a message. Writing of the September 11 attacks, an al-Qaeda spokesman declared, "It rang the bells of restoring Arab and Islamic glory."

Fourth, the act and the victim usually have symbolic significance. Bin Laden referred to the Twin Towers as "icons" of America's "military and economic power." The shock value of the act is enormously enhanced by the symbolism of the target. The whole point is for the psychological impact to be greater than the actual physical act. Terrorism is indeed a weapon of the weak. Terrorist movements are invariably both outmanned and outgunned by their opponents, so they employ such tactics in an effort to gain more attention than any objective assessment of their capabilities would suggest that they warrant.

Fifth—and this is a controversial point—terrorism is the act of substate groups, not states.

This is not to argue that states do not use terrorism as an instrument of foreign policy. We know they do. Many states, such as Iran, Iraq, Syria, and Libya, have sponsored terrorism abroad because they did not want to incur the risk of overtly attacking more powerful countries. Great powers have supported terrorist groups abroad as a way of engaging in proxy warfare or covertly bringing about internal change in difficult countries without openly displaying their strength. Nor do I wish to argue that states refrain from action that is the moral equivalent of terrorism. We know they don't. The Allied bombing campaign in World War II, culminating in the bombing of Hiroshima and Nagasaki, was a deliberate effort to target civilian populations in order to force the hand of their government. The policy of collective punishment visited on communities that produce terrorists is another example of targeting civilians to achieve a political purpose. Nevertheless, if we want to have any analytical clarity in understanding the behavior of terrorist groups, we must understand them as substate actors rather than states.

A sixth characteristic of terrorism is that the victim of the violence and the audience the terrorists are trying to reach are not the same. Victims are used as a means of altering the behavior of a larger audience, usually a government. Victims are chosen either at random or as representative of some larger group. Individual victims are interchangeable. The identities of the people traveling on a bus in Tel Aviv or a train in Madrid, dancing in Bali or bond trading in New York, were of no consequence to those who killed them. They were being used to influence others. This is different from most other forms of political violence, in which security forces or state representatives are targeted in an effort to reduce the strength of an opponent.

The final and most important defining characteristic of terrorism is the deliberate targeting of civilians. This is what sets terrorism apart from other forms of political violence, even the most proximate form, guerrilla warfare. Terrorists have elevated practices that are normally seen as the excesses of warfare to routine practice, striking noncombatants not as an unintended side effect but as deliberate strategy. They insist that those who pay taxes to a government are responsible for their actions whether they are Russians or Americans. Basayev declared all Russians fair game because "They pay taxes. They give approval in word and in deed. They are all responsible." Bin Laden similarly said of Americans, "He is the enemy of ours whether he fights us directly or merely pays his taxes." ...

THE RATIONALITY OF TERRORISM

We often think of terrorists as crazies. How can killing tourists at a shrine in Luxor or airline passengers in the United States possibly help the cause of Islamic fundamentalism? How can killing children in Beslan, shoppers in London, or tourists in Spain advance the cause of Chechen, Irish, or Basque nationalism? Terrorists must be deranged psychopaths. Their actions seem to make no sense.

But terrorists, by and large, are not insane at all. Their primary shared characteristic is their normalcy, insofar as we understand the term. Psychological studies of terrorists are virtually unanimous on this point. The British journalist Peter Taylor remembers asking a young prisoner from Derry, who was serving a life sentence for murder, what an IRA man was doing reading Tolstoy and Hardy. The prisoner replied, "Because an IRA man's normal like everyone else." When Taylor pointed out that normal people did not go around killing people, the prisoner replied that normal people elsewhere did not live in Northern Ireland. There are, of course, psychopaths to be found in many terrorist groups, as in many organizations in which violence is sanctioned. But there are not nearly as many psychopaths in terrorist groups as one might imagine.

Most organizations consider them a liability and quite deliberately try to select them out. This holds true across different types of groups, from ethnonationalists to religious fundamentalists.

Historically, terrorists have been very conservative in their choice of tactics. The most common terrorist act is a bombing, and it is not hard to see why. It is cheap. It is easy to get away from the scene of the attack. Moreover, it is dramatic and often indiscriminate. The notion that terrorists are mad has been advanced by the increasing use of suicide terrorism. But from an organizational point of view, suicide attacks are very rational, indeed economical. In the words of Dr. Ayman al-Zawahiri, bin Laden's second in command, "The method of martyrdom operation is the most successful way of inflicting damage against the opponent and least costly to the mujahedin in terms of casualties." It is also, of course, more effective.

Even if suicide terrorism makes sense from an organizational point of view, it seems insane from an individual point of view. But the organizations that employ the tactic have more volunteers than they need. They deliberately do not accept volunteers they consider depressed or suicidal. In the words of the Palestinian Fayez Jaber, an al-Aqsa commander who trained suicide bombers, "There are certain criteria that we observe. People with mental or psychological problems or personal family problems—I cannot allow myself to send such people. ... A person has to be a fully mature person, an adult, a sane person, and of course, not less than 18 years of age and fully aware of what he is about to carry out." Those who become martyrs appear to do so out of a combination of motives: anger, humiliation, a desire for revenge, commitment to their comrades and their cause, and a desire to attain glory—in other words, for reasons no more irrational than those of anyone prepared to give his life for a cause.

Terrorists' behavior has long seemed senseless to onlookers. The actions of the famous medieval sect the Assassins seemed so incomprehensible to others that for centuries it was believed that they were high on hashish when they undertook their suicide operations. It now appears that they were intoxicated only by their own ideology.

THE MORALITY OF TERRORISM

Another almost universally accepted attribute of terrorists is their amorality—in the words of President Bush, "abandoning every value except the will to power." Yet I have never met a terrorist who considered him/herself either immoral or amoral. Quite the contrary. When not acting as terrorists, they practice as much or as little morality in their daily lives as most of the rest of us. Most terrorists, moreover, go to considerable lengths to justify their actions on moral grounds, both in their public pronouncements and in their internal writings.

Albert Camus, in his play *Les Justes*, beautifully captures the sense of morality of the nineteenth-century anarchists, the precursors of many contemporary terrorists. He describes how Kaliayev, seeing two children seated in the carriage next to his intended target, the grand duke, could not bring himself to hurl the bomb. He subsequently does kill the grand duke and is executed, but he could not justify to himself killing children.

Many contemporary terrorists, of course, have no trouble justifying the killing of children. There are generally a number of defenses offered for the resort to terrorism. First, that it is entered into only as a last resort. Bin Laden made this claim in his 1996 fatwa, or declaration of war, against America: "Why is it then the regime closed all peaceful routes and pushed the people toward armed actions?!! Which is the only choice left for them to implement righteousness and justice." This is an empirical claim. As such, it can quickly be refuted with reference to the facts. Many terrorist groups do first try political action, but they have hardly exhausted the options available to them when they resort to terrorism.

The second common claim is that no other strategy is available. Vellupillai Prabakharan, the charismatic leader of the Tamil Tigers, put it succinctly: "We have no other option but to fight back." One member of al-Qassam, the military wing of Hamas, told the Pakistani writer and relief worker Nasra Hassan, "We do not have tanks or rockets, but we have something superior—our exploding human bombs." A young Italian *brigadista* spoke in similar terms: "I'm not a killer, I'm not a terrorist, I'm someone with a series of values, who wants to be active in politics, and today the only way ... to be politically active is this." If you are the twenty-five members of the Baader-Meinhof Gang in Germany and desire to overthrow the German capitalist state immediately, there are not too many options available. Ulrike Meinhof, in one of the first communiqués of the Baader-Meinhof Gang, declared that urban guerrilla warfare was "the only revolutionary method of intervention available to what are on the whole weak revolutionary forces." The problem with this argument is that there are always other options available. If those who seek change decided to take a longer time frame and embark on a protracted political strategy of propaganda and civil disobedience, they might undermine the state. But they want immediate results. So their weakness is in relationship to both the state and the broader population who do not share their views. If they had broader support, they wouldn't need to resort to terrorism. So terrorism may well be the only option available, but only if one lacks support, wants immediate results, and is prepared to murder innocents.

Third, those who commit terrorist acts often argue that terrorism works. Certainly the actions of Black September Palestinians, famous for hijacking airplanes and, most notoriously, for murdering members of the Israeli Olympic team in Munich in 1972, brought international attention to the plight of the Palestinians, just as IRA violence in Northern Ireland brought attention to the denial of civil rights to Northern Irish Catholics. But to prove that terrorism works, one would have to show that terrorism achieved what the terrorists wanted and what other means could not, and this has never been done. Maybe the IRA campaign and the ensuing loss of 3,500 lives in Northern Ireland has resulted in the power-sharing executive today in Northern Ireland, but this executive (currently suspended) is a far cry from the Irish unity the IRA has always demanded. Moreover, it is surely reasonable to expect that the same result could have been achieved through concerted peaceful political action over the past thirty years and without any significant loss of life.

The two most common arguments to justify the actions of contemporary Islamic fundamentalists are those of collective guilt and of moral equivalence. Palestinian radicals have long insisted that Israeli civilians, all of whom are obliged to serve in the country's security services, are not civilians and hence constitute legitimate targets: "They are not innocent if they are part of the total population, which is part of the army.... From 18 on, they are soldiers, even if they have civilian clothes." Similarly, bin Laden has argued explicitly that Americans and Western citizens have the option of changing their governments and when they do not are responsible for their actions. He declared, "The American people are the ones who pay the taxes which fund the planes that bomb us in Afghanistan, the tanks that strike and destroy our homes in Pakistan, the armies which occupy our lands in the Arabian Gulf, and the fleets which ensure the blockade of Iraq."

The final argument is the familiar teenage response: "Everybody does it." Our terrorism is justified because everyone else practices terrorism too. An angry Palestinian told Nasra Hassan, "The Israelis kill our children and our women. This is war, and innocent people get hurt." Eddie Kinner, a young Protestant paramilitary in Northern Ireland, used similar language: "As far as I was concerned, I had joined an army and we were engaged in a war. The enemy had attacked my community and I was prepared to respond in kind." In all his statements bin Laden goes into detail about the iniquities of the United States, the bombing of Hiroshima and Nagasaki, the killing of Iraqi children with U.S. sanctions and Afghan villagers with U.S. bombs. He and his followers believe that the United States lives by force and so they must respond with force. Bin Laden declared long before 9/11, "Through history America has not been known to differentiate between the military and the civilians, between men and women, or adults and children. Those who hurled atomic bombs and used the weapons of mass destruction against Nagasaki and Hiroshima were the Americans. Can the bombs differentiate between military and women and infants and children?"

Even when arguing that it is legitimate to kill civilians and that they are doing to their enemies only what their enemies are doing to them, they continue to impose limits on the degree to which they can inflict harm on their enemies. Ramzi bin al-Shibh, one of the masterminds of the 9/11 attacks, who was arrested in Karachi, Pakistan, on September 11, 2002, composed an ideological justification of the September 11, 2001, attacks intended for internal consumption. He wrote:

> Because of Saddam and the Baath Party, America punished a whole population. Thus its bombs and its embargo killed millions of Iraqi Muslims. And because of Osama bin Laden, America surrounded Afghans and bombed them, causing the death of tens of thousands of Muslims.... God said to assault whoever assaults you, in a like manner.... In killing Americans who are ordinarily off limits, Muslims should not exceed four million non-combatants, or render more than ten million of them homeless. We should avoid this, to make sure the penalty is no more than reciprocal.

The fact that a senior al-Qaeda operative feels justified in killing four million Americans and making ten million homeless is hardly grounds for optimism, but it does demonstrate that al-Qaeda does have a code that imposes restraints on its actions. As bin Laden has said, "Reciprocal treatment is fair." The constant declarations of war by fatwa are another attempt to appeal to a higher authority to justify their actions.

Finally, the popularity of suicide attacks, or "martyrdom operations," as those who volunteer prefer to call them, is in itself a moral claim. Our fascination with suicide attack is due to a number of factors: our fear of its destructiveness, our sense that it is crazy and therefore incomprehensible, and, finally, our discomfiture that it doesn't quite sit well with our sense of terrorists as depraved. Part of the popularity of the act among terrorists is, indeed, its destructiveness, but volunteers are also attracted precisely because it is an assertion of a claim to moral superiority over the enemy.

This is most obviously the case for hunger strikers. The tradition of inflicting harm on oneself in an effort to shame one's enemy has a long history in many cultures, and particularly the Gaelic one. When ten imprisoned republican prisoners slowly starved themselves to death in 1981, they were denying the depiction of them as depraved criminals. They were in fact claiming the moral high ground. It was also an enormously effective tactic. Even if they did not thereby gain the immediate goal, political prisoner status, they won worldwide attention and more new recruits than the movement could manage. The popular sympathy was such that one of the hunger strikers was elected to Parliament in a landslide.

It is, of course, easier to justify killing oneself for a cause than killing oneself as a means of killing others, especially when those others are civilians going about their daily lives. Nevertheless, the scores of young men, and increasingly young women and older men, who volunteer for suicide operations do so believing that they are acting morally, selflessly giving their lives for a cause. In one video, made on the eve of a suicide attack on an Israeli bus, a member of Hamas says, "We want to make it clear to the world that the true killer is Israel because our demands are legitimate."

Terrorists are substate actors who violently target noncombatants to communicate a political message to a third party. Terrorists are neither crazy nor amoral. They come from all parts of the world. They come from many walks of life. They fight for a range of different causes. Some have support from the communities from which they come; some do not. They range in size from a handful of Corsican nationalists to thousands of armed Tamils. Some are fighting for the same goals that have motivated wars for centuries, such as control over national territory. Some are trying to overthrow the state system itself. They come from all religious traditions and from none. One thing they do have in common: they are weaker than those they oppose.

REVIEW QUESTIONS

1. How does Richardson define terrorism? What are its characteristics?
2. Why does Richardson reject the claim that terrorists are insane?
3. How do terrorists defend the morality of their actions according to Richardson?

DISCUSSION QUESTIONS

1. Is terrorism immoral? Why or why not?
2. Do states commit acts of terrorism? Were the nuclear attacks on Hiroshima and Nagaski, which deliberately and violently targeted civilians for political purposes, acts of terrorism? What is your view?

Questions Regarding a War on Terrorism

CLAUDIA CARD

Claudia Card is Emma Goldman Professor of Philosophy at the University of Wisconsin, and affiliate professor in Jewish Studies, Women's Studies, and Environmental Studies. From 2002 to 2007, she was senior fellow at the Institute for Research in the Humanities at the

Source: "Questions Regarding a War on Terrorism" by Claudia Card from *Hypatia*, Vol. 18, No. 1, pp. 164–169. Reprinted by permission of Indiana University Press.

University of Wisconsin, where she is writing a book on responding to atrocities. She is the author of *The Atrocity Paradigm* (2002), *The Unnatural Lottery* (1996), *Lesbian Choices* (1995), and more than 100 articles and reviews. She is the editor of *The Cambridge Companion to Beauvoir* (2003), *On Feminist Ethics and Politics* (1999), *Adventures in Lesbian Philosophy* (1994), and *Feminist Ethics* (1991).

Card thinks it is clear that the 9/11 attacks were terrorist and evil. Less clear is how to respond. Declaring a war on terrorism is problematic. It gives the attacks an appearance of legitimacy they do not deserve. It is not a war in the usual sense, and it cannot be just war on the principles of just war theory. Indeed, the war on terrorism seems to violate the principle that criminals should be given a trial; it steps outside the rules of international law. This is not to say that no response to the 9/11 attacks is appropriate. Care suggests global hunts for those responsible for the planning and support and trials by international tribunals.

Unlike some critics, I do not have great moral difficulty in identifying as terrorist and as evil the bombing attacks on the World Trade Center on September 11, 2001. Regardless of perpetrators' grievances and their understandings of their religious commitments or aspirations, mass killing of unarmed civilians targeted deliberately as such and without warning is evil. On Carl Wellman's widely received view of terrorism as political violence with two targets, one direct (but secondary target) who suffers immediate harm and the other an indirect (but primary) target to whom a message is sent by way of that harm, the attacks were also terrorist if their larger intent was to manipulate the United States government politically (Wellman 1979, 254).[1]

No one has yet publicly claimed responsibility for the attacks or offered an official explanation. And so we can only infer the larger intent. But evidence shows the attacks, including the surprise element, to have been planned (Reporters, Writers, and Editors of Der Spiegel 2002). This was no ordinary wrong. If evils are intolerable harms that were reasonably foreseeable (if not planned) and produced by culpable wrongdoing, these events appear to be paradigmatic evils (Card 2002).[2]

Philosophically less clear is whether the response of a war on terrorism is not also an evil. Without resolving that question I mention issues that make it unclear and suggest a way to address particular cases. More importantly, in drawing on an analogy with terrorism in the home, I suggest an alternative, preferable response that would make such a determination unnecessary.

Some may regard the expression "war on terrorism" as metaphorical, like the expressions "war on drugs" or "war on crime." Yet "war" here confers an appearance of legitimacy, conveys that lesser means were tried and exhausted, and dignifies the original attack as an act of war, rather than simply an atrocious crime. How metaphorical is it, one may wonder, when military forces are deployed to carry out the war? Despite the dropping of food and supplies for civilians, U.S. armed forces have inflicted intolerable harm, including much death, on people in Afghanistan, including many unarmed women and children. Whether that is evil depends on whether those intolerable harms were reasonably foreseeable and perpetrated through culpable wrongdoing.

Whether war can be a legitimate response to attacks carried out by persons unauthorized by any state raises philosophical issues about the meaning of war and questions about the justice of a military force response, whatever we call it. Is war on terrorism within the bounds of what justice permits as a response to the attacks of 9–11? What *are* the boundaries, the limits, of a "war on terrorism?" In particular, how is the scope of this war's *opponents* limited?

Appropriate responses to 9–11, in my view, would include global hunts (with international cooperation) for responsible survivors, those complicit in the planning and support of the attacks, including the provision of training, financial backing, and safe harbors. Persons apprehended would ideally then be tried by international tribunals, treated as (suspected) criminal agents, charged with crimes against humanity for targeting victims on the basis of their (perceived) identity as Americans, American sympathizers, or as capitalists.[3] Universal jurisdiction applies for crimes against humanity (Gutman and Rieff 1999, 108). Still, an international court would be more appropriate, as those killed in the World Trade Center represented many nations. The deed threatens security globally. Although suspects may try to avoid being taken alive, pursuers can aim to take them alive and try them. If war is declared rather than a hunt for responsible individuals, who has the opportunity for a fair trial?

War, according to *Merriam Webster's Collegiate Dictionary Tenth Edition,* is "a state of usually open and declared armed hostile conflict between states or nations" (s.v. "war"). Internationally accepted rules of war have evolved to regulate wars *with* or *between* opponents. What guidelines regulate wars *on* or *against* such "opponents" as terrorism or drugs? By tradition, a just war must be declared by appropriate authorities. A major point of this requirement is to give fair notice to opponents. On whom is a war on "terrorism" declared? Who is given fair notice? In wars between states, heads of state can negotiate for peace. Who among the opponents in a war on terrorism has authority to negotiate for peace? If peace is not negotiable, how must such a war end? What is to prevent it from becoming a war of extermination?

According to just war theory, a principle of discrimination between combatants and noncombatants holds that it is unjust to target civilians directly. It is unjust to kill civilians simply for the sake of demoralizing one's opponent, for example. Such a policy violates Immanuel Kant's principle that humanity in anyone's person must never be treated merely as a means but must be treated always at the same time as an end (Kant 1996, 80). Modern warfare makes it nearly impossible to use weapons such as bombs against combatants without risking lives of noncombatants. Still, the principle of discrimination is not empty as long as it rules out deliberately targeting civilians when risking their lives is not a consequence of using weapons against combatants. But whom is it unjust to target directly in a war on terrorism?

Members of nations at war who wear a military uniform are identifiable as combatants; those who do not are presumed civilians. Guerilla warfare, of course, complicates this distinction, as guerilla combatants wear no uniform. Wars against opponents who are not nations raise more complications. What corresponds to "civilian" in the party to a war that is not a nation or state? What must one's relationship to acts of terrorism be in order for one to count as a terrorist?

"Terrorists" is not a well-defined group. "Terrorist" is not an identity, like British or French. To identify someone as a terrorist is to render a judgment on them, not simply to make a discovery. Not all terrorists have common goals, belong to a unified organization, or have the same opponents. There are terrorists within the United States who are U.S. citizens and not immigrants, legal or illegal. The Ku Klux Klan is one of the most infamous of terrorist organizations, and the era of lynching is one of the most infamous episodes of domestic terrorism in U.S. history.

Other domestic terrorists are less widely or publicly acknowledged as such. The reigning stereotype of a terrorist is one who, in seeking attention for national or international political causes, carries out destructive acts against public institutions or in public places. This stereotype ignores not only state terrorism, as Jonathan Glover, Emma Goldman, and others have pointed out, but it also ignores the terrorism of violence in the home (Glover 1991; Goldman 1969; Card 1991). Such violence in the home functions to maintain dominance (usually patriarchal) and thereby can be acknowledged as political. A truly global war on terrorism would include among its targets perpetrators of domestic partner abuse, elder abuse, child abuse, and rape. President Bush has not yet recognized such perpetrators as terrorists. They do not appear to be among his targets. But for those who would support a war on terrorism, it should be an interesting question whether war would be an appropriate response to terrorists in the home.

If the United States is justified in conducting a war on international terrorists, should feminists declare war on terrorism in the home? Should battered women (and likewise battered children and battered elders) regard themselves as existing in a state of nature—as though laws, courts, and governments did not exist—with respect to batterers? After years of stalking and battering by her former husband, against whom the law either would not or could not protect her and her children, Francine Hughes poured gasoline over her batterer one night and ignited it while he slept (McNulty 1980). If killing without capture and trial is clearly an appropriate response to international terrorists, should Francine Hughes even have been put on trial for murder?

It will be objected that feminists and victims of battery are not in positions of authority to undertake such matters as declaring war. Yet why is the issue of authority important, if not as part of a broader understanding of rules defining conditions under which fighting is fair? Have not such rules been abandoned already, if opponents are not sufficiently well-defined that one can identify who has authority to negotiate for peace? Is the real objection that the victims of terrorism in the home are usually female and that war is not an appropriate response for females?

When terrorists disregard fairness, victims face a difficult question: to what extent ought one to be fair even to those who disregard fairness themselves? Domestic criminals often enough blatantly disregard fairness. Yet the state offers them a trial. Trials are reassuring to others not accused in a particular case, as they might one day be mistakenly identified as criminals, in which case a fair trial would give them the opportunity to rebut the charge. Striking back without trial, on the assumption that those who are unfair to others do not deserve fairness, ignores the possibility that retaliators might be mistaken in their judgments about those identified as criminal (mistaken either about what was done or about who did it). The same point applies to international terrorism. Without trials by international tribunals, what assurance do citizens of the world have that they will not be mistakenly identified as terrorists and summarily dispatched? Some arguments analogous to these were offered in support of the International Tribunal at Nuremberg against

those who advocated simply shooting those identified by the Allies as Axis leaders at the end of World War II (Taylor 1992).

It was unfortunate but nevertheless right to try Francine Hughes and to make public the facts that led her to the deed. A trial is the right way to determine whether her response was justified, and if so, to clear her name. It would have been morally right to acquit her, even without the insanity defense, given her history of having exhausted less desperate methods of self-defense.[4] She should never have been left in the position of having to defend herself by extreme means. The man she killed is the person who, ideally, should have had to stand trial.

If a nation declares a war on terrorism, rather than on another nation, it takes matters into its own hands in a manner that is in some respects analogous to what Francine Hughes did. It steps outside the bounds and processes of law—in this case, international law. Of course, Francine Hughes appears not to have warned her opponent, who was asleep and therefore unable to try to escape. A state may warn terrorists by declaring war. But if "terrorist" is not well-defined (and the reader may notice by now that I have not really defined it; it is currently a hotly contested concept, which is part of the point), who knows that they are being warned? If everyone in a territory that includes terrorists is warned, of what value is the warning when many inhabitants who are not terrorists have no means of escape or self-defense?

If it was right for the state of Michigan to try Francine Hughes for murder (which as stated above, I believe it was), then perhaps it would also be right, and for similar reasons, for an international tribunal to try, for crimes against humanity, the leaders of nations who declare and perpetrate war on terrorists, when those nations kill masses of unarmed civilians. Such a trial may be the right way to determine whether the war was justified, and if so, to clear the names of nations who wage it. Such a trial should also offer some reassurance to others who might one day be wrongly identified as terrorists. It would consider, for example, whether less drastic but appropriate responses had been exhausted by any nation that wages a war allegedly on terrorism in which it kills masses of unarmed civilians who have no means of escape.

Would it not make better sense, however, for an international team to capture and try, in an international court, those initially accused of international terrorism and or of being complicit in it, just as it would have made better sense to capture and try the batterer of Francine Hughes?

NOTES

1. By citing these two targets, Wellman distinguishes terrorism from torture, which need have no ulterior motive but may be inflicted simply as sadism or revenge.

2. For development of the theory that evils are reasonably foreseeable intolerable harms produced by culpable wrongdoing, see Card 2002.

3. Crimes against humanity are understood as acts of violence "against an identifiable group of persons, irrespective of the make-up of that group or the purpose of the persecution" (Gutman and Rieff 1999, 107). Regarding it as a crime against humanity to kill individuals just because they are (perceived to be) capitalists does not presuppose an endorsement of judgment about the value of being a capitalist.

4. According to McNulty (1980), under Michigan law, there was no other way to acquit Francine Hughes of murder than to use the insanity defense, although many would be inclined to say that the crime with which she was charged was perhaps one of the sanest deeds of her life.

REFERENCES

Card, Claudia. 1991. "Rape as a terrorist institution." In *Violence, terrorism, and justice,* ed. R. G. Frey and Christopher W. Morris. Cambridge: Cambridge University Press.

——.2002. *The atrocity paradigm: A theory of evil.* New York: Oxford University Press.

Glover, Jonathan. 1991. State terrorism. In *Violence, terrorism, and justice,* ed. R. G. Frey and Christopher W. Morris. Cambridge: Cambridge University Press.

Goldman, Emma. 1969. The psychology of political violence. In *Goldman, Anarchism and other essays.* New York: Dover.

Gutman, Roy, and David Rieff, eds.1999. *Crimes of war. What the public should know.* New York: Norton.

Kant, Immanuel. 1996. *Groundwork of the metaphysics of morals.* In *Practical philosophy,* trans. and ed. Mary J. Gregor. Cambridge: Cambridge University Press.

McNulty, Faith. 1980. *The burning bed.* New York: Harcourt Brace Jovanovich.

Reporters, Writers, and Editors of *Der Spiegel.* 2001. *Inside 9–11: What really happened.* New York: St. Martin's Press.

Taylor, Telford. 1992. *Anatomy of the Nuremberg trials: A personal memoir.* New York: Knopf.

Wellman, Carl. 1979. On terrorism itself. *Journal of Value Inquiry* (13): 241–49.

REVIEW QUESTIONS

1. Why does Card think that the 9/11 attacks were terrorist and evil?
2. Explain Card's objections to the expression "war on terrorism."
3. What are appropriate responses to the 9/11 attacks in Card's view?
4. How does the dictionary define war? What problems does this definition raise for the war on terrorism according to Card?
5. What point is Card making with the case of Francine Hughes?

DISCUSSION QUESTIONS

1. What is an appropriate response to the 9/11 attacks? Is the war on terrorism an appropriate response? Why or why not?
2. Is the case of Francine Hughes analogous to cases where suspected terrorists are killed? Explain your view.

The War on Terrorism and the End of Human Rights

DAVID LUBAN

David Luban is the Frederick J. Hass Professor of Law and Philosophy at the Georgetown University Law Center. He is the author of *Lawyers and Justice* (1988), *Legal Modernism* (1994), *Legal Ethics and Human Dignity* (2007), and numerous journal articles and book chapters.

Luban argues that the current War on Terrorism combines a war model with a law model to produce a new model of state action, a hybrid war-law model. This hybrid model selectively picks out elements of the war and law models to maximize the use of lethal force while eliminating the rights of both adversaries and innocent bystanders. The result is that the War on Terrorism means the end of human rights.

In the immediate aftermath of September 11, President Bush stated that the perpetrators of the deed would be brought to justice. Soon afterwards, the President announced that the United States would engage in a war on terrorism. The first of these statements adopts the familiar language of criminal law and criminal justice. It treats the September 11 attacks as horrific crimes—mass murders—and the government's mission as apprehending and punishing the surviving planners and conspirators for their roles in the crimes. The War on Terrorism is a different proposition, however, and a different model of governmental action—not law but war. Most obviously, it dramatically broadens the scope of action, because now terrorists who knew nothing about September 11 have been earmarked as enemies. But that is only the beginning.

THE HYBRID WAR-LAW APPROACH

The model of war offers much freer rein than that of law, and therein lies its appeal in the wake of 9/11. First, in war but not in law it is permissible to use lethal force on enemy troops regardless of their degree of personal involvement with the adversary. The conscripted cook is as legitimate a target as the enemy general. Second, in war but not in law "collateral damage," that is, foreseen but unintended killing of noncombatants, is permissible. (Police cannot blow up an apartment building full of people because a murderer is inside, but an air force can bomb the building if it contains a military target.) Third, the requirements of evidence and proof are drastically weaker in war than in criminal justice. Soldiers do not need proof beyond a reasonable doubt, or even proof by a preponderance of evidence, that someone is an enemy soldier before firing on him or capturing and imprisoning him. They don't need proof at all, merely plausible intelligence. Thus, the U.S. military remains regretful but unapologetic about its January 2002 attack on the Afghani town of Uruzgan, in which 21 innocent civilians were killed, based on faulty intelligence that they were al Qaeda fighters. Fourth, in war one can attack an enemy without concern over whether he has done anything. Legitimate targets are those who in the course of combat *might* harm us, not those who *have* harmed us. No doubt there are other significant differences as well. But the basic point should be clear: Given Washington's mandate to eliminate the danger of future 9/11s, so far as humanly possible, the model of war offers important advantages over the model of law.

There are disadvantages as well. Most obviously, in war but not in law, fighting back is a *legitimate* response of the enemy. Second, when nations fight a war, other nations may opt for neutrality. Third, because fighting back is legitimate, in war the enemy soldier deserves special regard once he is rendered harmless through injury or surrender. It is impermissible to punish him for his role in fighting the war. Nor can he be harshly interrogated after he is captured. The Third Geneva Convention provides: "Prisoners of war who refuse to answer [questions] may not be threatened, insulted, or exposed to unpleasant or disadvantageous treatment of any kind." And, when the war concludes, the enemy soldier must be repatriated.

Here, however, Washington has different ideas, designed to eliminate these tactical disadvantages in the traditional war model. Washington regards international terrorism not only as a military adversary, but also as a criminal activity and criminal conspiracy. In the law model, criminals don't get to shoot back, and their acts of violence subject them to legitimate punishment. That is what we see in Washington's prosecution of the War on Terrorism. Captured terrorists may be tried before military or civilian tribunals, and shooting back at Americans, including American troops, is a federal crime (for a statute under which John Walker Lindh was indicted criminalizes anyone regardless of nationality, who "outside the United States attempts to kill, or engages in a conspiracy to kill, a national of the United States" or "engages in physical violence with intent to cause serious bodily injury to a national of the United States; or with the result that serious bodily injury is caused to a national of the United States"). Furthermore, the U.S. may rightly demand that other countries not be neutral about murder and terrorism. Unlike the war model, a nation may insist that those who are not with us in fighting murder and terror are

against us, because by not joining our operations they are providing a safe haven for terrorists or their bank accounts. By selectively combining elements of the war model and elements of the law model, Washington is able to maximize its own ability to mobilize lethal force against terrorists while eliminating most traditional rights of a military adversary, as well as the rights of innocent bystanders caught in the crossfire.

A LIMBO OF RIGHTLESSNESS

The legal status of al Qaeda suspects imprisoned at the Guantanamo Bay Naval Base in Cuba is emblematic of this hybrid war-law approach to the threat of terrorism. In line with the war model, they lack the usual rights of criminal suspects—the presumption of innocence, the right to a hearing to determine guilt, the opportunity to prove that the authorities have grabbed the wrong man. But, in line with the law model, they are considered *unlawful* combatants. Because they are not uniformed forces, they lack the rights of prisoners of war and are liable to criminal punishment. Initially, the American government declared that the Guantanamo Bay prisoners have no rights under the Geneva Conventions. In the face of international protests, Washington quickly backpedaled and announced that the Guantanamo Bay prisoners would indeed be treated as decently as POWs—but it also made clear that the prisoners have no right to such treatment. Neither criminal suspects nor POWs, neither fish nor fowl, they inhabit a limbo of rightlessness. Secretary of Defense Rumsfeld's assertion that the U.S. may continue to detain them even if they are acquitted by a military tribunal dramatizes the point.

To understand how extraordinary their status is, consider an analogy. Suppose that Washington declares a War on Organized Crime. Troops are dispatched to Sicily, and a number of Mafiosi are seized, brought to Guantanamo Bay, and imprisoned without a hearing for the indefinite future, maybe the rest of their lives. They are accused of no crimes, because their capture is based not on what they have done but on what they might do. After all, to become "made" they took oaths of obedience to the bad guys. Seizing them accords with the war model: they are enemy foot soldiers. But they are foot soldiers out of uniform; they lack a "fixed distinctive emblem," in the words of The Hague Convention. That makes them unlawful combatants, so they lack the rights of POWs. They may object that it is only a unilateral declaration by the American President that has turned them into combatants in the first place—he called it a war, they didn't—and that, since they do not regard themselves as literal foot soldiers it never occurred to them to wear a fixed distinctive emblem. They have a point. It seems too easy for the President to divest anyone in the world of rights and liberty simply by announcing that the U.S. is at war with them and then declaring them unlawful combatants if they resist. But, in the hybrid war-law model, they protest in vain.

Consider another example. In January 2002, U.S. forces in Bosnia seized five Algerians and a Yemeni suspected of al Qaeda connections and took them to Guantanamo Bay. The six had been jailed in Bosnia, but a Bosnian court released them for lack of evidence, and the Bosnian Human Rights Chamber issued an injunction that four of them be allowed to remain in the country pending further legal proceedings. The Human Rights Chamber, ironically, was created under U.S. auspices in the Dayton peace accords, and it was designed specifically to protect against treatment like this. Ruth Wedgwood, a well-known international law scholar at Yale and a member of the Council on Foreign Relations, defended the Bosnian seizure in war-model terms. "I think we would simply argue this was a matter of self-defense. One of the fundamental rules of military law is that you have a right ultimately to act in self-defense. And if these folks were actively plotting to blow up the U.S. embassy, they should be considered combatants and captured as combatants in a war." Notice that Professor Wedgwood argues in terms of what the men seized in Bosnia were *planning to do,* not what they *did;* notice as well that the decision of the Bosnian court that there was insufficient evidence does not matter. These are characteristics of the war model.

More recently, two American citizens alleged to be al Qaeda operatives (Jose Padilla, a.k.a. Abdullah al Muhajir, and Yasser Esam Hamdi) have been held in American military prisons, with no crimes charged, no opportunity to consult counsel, and no hearing. The President described Padilla as "a bad man" who aimed to build a nuclear "dirty" bomb and use it against America; and the Justice Department has classified both men as "enemy combatants" who may be held indefinitely. Yet, as military law expert Gary Solis points out, "Until now, as used by the attorney general, the term 'enemy combatant' appeared nowhere in U.S. criminal law, international law or in the law of war." The phrase comes from the 1942 Supreme Court case *Ex parte Quirin,* but all the Court says there is that "an enemy combatant who without uniform comes secretly through the lines for the purpose of waging war by destruction of life or property" would "not . . . be entitled to the status of prisoner of war, but . . . [they would] be offenders against the law of war subject to trial and punishment by military tribunals." For the Court, in other words, the status of a person as a non-uniformed enemy combatant makes him a criminal rather than a warrior, and determines *where* he is tried (in a military, rather than a civilian, tribunal) but not *whether* he is tried. Far from authorizing open-ended confinement, *Ex parte Quirin* presupposes that criminals are entitled to hearings: without a hearing how can suspects prove that the government made a mistake? *Quirin* embeds the concept of "enemy combatant" firmly in the law model. In the war model, by contrast, POWs may be detained without a hearing until hostilities are over. But POWs were captured in uniform, and only their undoubted identity as enemy soldiers justifies such open-ended custody. Apparently, Hamdi and Padilla will get the worst of both models—open-ended custody with no trial, like POWs, but no certainty beyond the U.S. government's say-so that they really are "bad men." This is the hybrid war-law model. It combines the *Quirin* category of "enemy combatant without uniform," used in the law model to justify a military trial, with the war model's practice of indefinite confinement with no trial at all.

THE CASE FOR THE HYBRID APPROACH

Is there any justification for the hybrid war-law model, which so drastically diminishes the rights of the enemy? An argument can be offered along the following lines. In ordinary cases of war among states, enemy soldiers may well be morally and politically innocent. Many of them are conscripts, and those who aren't do not necessarily endorse the state policies they are fighting to defend. But enemy soldiers in the War on Terrorism are, by definition, those who have embarked on a path of terrorism. They are neither morally nor politically innocent. Their sworn aim—"Death to America!"—is to create more 9/11s. In this respect, they are much more akin to criminal conspirators than to conscript soldiers. Terrorists will fight as soldiers when they must, and metamorphose into mass murderers when they can.

Furthermore, suicide terrorists pose a special, unique danger. Ordinary criminals do not target innocent bystanders. They may be willing to kill them if necessary, but bystanders enjoy at least some measure of security because they are not primary targets. Not so with terrorists, who aim to kill as many innocent people as possible. Likewise, innocent bystanders are protected from ordinary criminals by whatever deterrent force the threat of punishment and the risk of getting killed in the act of committing a crime offer. For a suicide bomber, neither of these threats is a deterrent at all—after all, for the suicide bomber one of the hallmarks of a *successful* operation is that he winds up dead at day's end. Given the unique and heightened danger that suicide terrorists pose, a stronger response that grants potential terrorists fewer rights may be justified. Add to this the danger that terrorists may come to possess weapons of mass destruction, including nuclear devices in suitcases. Under circumstances of such dire menace, it is appropriate to treat terrorists as though they embody the most dangerous aspects of both warriors and criminals. That is the basis of the hybrid war-law model.

THE CASE AGAINST EXPEDIENCY

The argument against the hybrid war-law model is equally clear. The U.S. has simply chosen the bits of the law model and the bits of the war model that are most convenient for American interests, and ignored the rest. The model abolishes the rights of potential enemies (and their innocent shields) by fiat—not for reasons of moral or legal principle, but solely because the U.S. does not want them to have rights. The more rights they have, the more risk they pose. But Americans' urgent desire to minimize our risks doesn't make other people's rights disappear. Calling our policy a War on Terrorism obscures this point.

The theoretical basis of the objection is that the law model and the war model each comes as a package, with a kind of intellectual integrity. The law model grows out of relationships within states, while the war model arises from relationships between states. The law model imputes a ground-level community of values to those subject to the law—paradigmatically, citizens of a state, but also visitors and foreigners who choose to engage in conduct that affects a state. Only because law imputes shared basic values to the community can a state condemn the conduct of criminals and inflict punishment on them. Criminals deserve condemnation and punishment because their conduct violates norms that we are entitled to count on their sharing. But, for the same reason—the imputed community of values—those subject to the law ordinarily enjoy a presumption of innocence and an expectation of safety. The government cannot simply grab them and confine them without making sure they have broken the law, nor can it condemn them without due process for ensuring that it has the right person, nor can it knowingly place bystanders in mortal peril in the course of fighting crime. They are our fellows, and the community should protect them just as it protects us. The same imputed community of values that justifies condemnation and punishment creates rights to due care and due process.

War is different. War is the ultimate acknowledgment that human beings do not live in a single community with shared norms. If their norms conflict enough, communities pose a physical danger to each other, and nothing can safeguard a community against its enemies except force of arms. That makes enemy soldiers legitimate targets; but it makes our soldiers legitimate targets as well, and, once the enemy no longer poses a danger, he should be immune from punishment, because if he has fought cleanly he has violated no norms that we are entitled to presume he honors. Our norms are, after all, *our* norms, not his.

Because the law model and war model come as conceptual packages, it is unprincipled to wrench them apart and recombine them simply because it is in America's interest to do so. To declare that Americans can fight enemies with the latitude of warriors, but if the enemies fight back they are not warriors but criminals, amounts to a kind of heads-I-win-tails-you-lose international morality in which whatever it takes to reduce American risk, no matter what the cost to others, turns out to be justified. This, in brief, is the criticism of the hybrid war-law model.

To be sure, the law model could be made to incorporate the war model merely by rewriting a handful of statutes. Congress could enact laws permitting imprisonment or execution of persons who pose a significant threat of terrorism whether or not they have already done anything wrong. The standard of evidence could be set low and the requirement of a hearing eliminated. Finally, Congress could authorize the use of lethal force against terrorists regardless of the danger to innocent bystanders, and it could immunize officials from lawsuits or prosecution by victims of collateral damage. Such statutes would violate the Constitution, but the Constitution could be amended to incorporate anti-terrorist exceptions to the Fourth, Fifth, and Sixth Amendments. In the end, we would have a system of law that includes all the essential features of the war model.

It would, however, be a system that imprisons people for their intentions rather than their actions, and that offers the innocent few protections against mistaken detention or inadvertent death through collateral damage. Gone are the principles that people should never be punished for their thoughts, only for their deeds, and that innocent people must be protected rather than injured by their own government. In that sense, at any rate, repackaging war as law seems merely cosmetic, because it replaces the ideal of law as a protector of rights with the more problematic goal of protecting some innocent people by sacrificing others. The hypothetical legislation incorporates war into law only by making law as partisan and ruthless as war. It no longer resembles law as Americans generally understand it.

THE THREAT TO INTERNATIONAL HUMAN RIGHTS

In the War on Terrorism, what becomes of international human rights? It seems beyond dispute that the war model poses a threat to international human rights, because honoring human rights is neither practically possible nor theoretically required during war. Combatants are legitimate targets; non-combatants maimed by accident or mistake are regarded as collateral damage rather than victims of atrocities; cases of mistaken identity get killed or confined without a hearing because combat conditions preclude due process. To be sure, the laws of war specify minimum human rights, but these are far less robust than rights in peacetime—and the hybrid war-law model reduces this schedule of rights even further by classifying the enemy as unlawful combatants.

One striking example of the erosion of human rights is tolerance of torture. It should be recalled that a 1995 al Qaeda plot to bomb eleven U.S. airliners was thwarted by information tortured out of a Pakistani suspect by the Philippine police—an eerie real-life version of the familiar philosophical thought-experiment. The *Washington Post* reports that since September 11 the U.S. has engaged in the summary transfer of dozens of terrorism suspects to countries where they will be interrogated under torture. But it isn't just the United States that has proven willing to tolerate torture for security reasons. Last December, the Swedish government snatched a suspected Islamic extremist to whom it had previously granted political asylum, and the same day had him transferred to Egypt, where Amnesty International reports that he has been tortured to the point where he walks only with difficulty. Sweden is not, to say the least, a traditionally hard-line nation on human rights issues. None of this international transportation is lawful—indeed, it violates international treaty obligations under the Convention against Torture that in the U.S. have constitutional status as "supreme Law of the Land"—but that may not matter under the war model, in which even constitutional rights may be abrogated.

It is natural to suggest that this suspension of human rights is an exceptional emergency measure to deal with an unprecedented threat. This raises the question of how long human rights will remain suspended. When will the war be over?

Here, the chief problem is that the War on Terrorism is not like any other kind of war. The enemy, Terrorism, is not a territorial state or nation or government. There is no opposite number to negotiate with. There is no one on the other side to call a truce or declare a cease-fire, no one among the enemy authorized to surrender. In traditional wars among states, the war aim is, as Clausewitz argued, to impose one state's political will on another's. The *aim* of the war is not to kill the enemy—killing the enemy is the *means* used to achieve the real end, which is to force capitulation. In the War on Terrorism, no capitulation is possible. That means that the real aim of the war is, quite simply, to kill or capture all of the terrorists—to keep on killing and killing, capturing and capturing, until they are all gone.

Of course, no one expects that terrorism will ever disappear completely. Everyone understands that new anti-American extremists, new terrorists, will always arise and always be available for recruitment and deployment. Everyone

understands that even if al Qaeda is destroyed or decapitated, other groups, with other leaders, will arise in its place. It follows, then, that the War on Terrorism will be a war that can only be abandoned, never concluded. The War has no natural resting point, no moment of victory or finality. It requires a mission of killing and capturing, in territories all over the globe, that will go on in perpetuity. It follows as well that the suspension of human rights implicit in the hybrid war-law model is not temporary but permanent.

Perhaps with this fear in mind, Congressional authorization of President Bush's military campaign limits its scope to those responsible for September 11 and their sponsors. But the War on Terrorism has taken on a life of its own that makes the Congressional authorization little more than a technicality. Because of the threat of nuclear terror, the American leadership actively debates a war on Iraq regardless of whether Iraq was implicated in September 11; and the President's yoking of Iraq, Iran, and North Korea into a single axis of evil because they back terror suggests that the War on Terrorism might eventually encompass all these nations. If the U.S. ever unearths tangible evidence that any of these countries is harboring or abetting terrorists with weapons of mass destruction, there can be little doubt that Congress will support military action. So too, Russia invokes the American War on Terrorism to justify its attacks on Chechen rebels, China uses it to deflect criticisms of its campaign against Uighur separatists, and Israeli Prime Minister Sharon explicitly links military actions against Palestinian insurgents to the American War on Terrorism. No doubt there is political opportunism at work in some or all of these efforts to piggy-back onto America's campaign, but the opportunity would not exist if "War on Terrorism" were merely the code-name of a discrete, neatly-boxed American operation. Instead, the War on Terrorism has become a model of politics, a world-view with its own distinctive premises and consequences. As I have argued, it includes a new model of state action, the hybrid war-law model, which depresses human rights from their peace-time standard to the war-time standard, and indeed even further. So long as it continues, the War on Terrorism means the end of human rights, at least for those near enough to be touched by the fire of battle.

Sources: On the January 2002 attack on the Afghani town of Uruzgan, see: John Ward Anderson, "Afghans Falsely Held by U.S. Tried to Explain; Fighters Recount Unanswered Pleas, Beatings—and an Apology on Their Release," *Washington Post* (March 26, 2002); see also Susan B. Glasser, "Afghans Live and Die With U.S. Mistakes; Villagers Tell of Over 100 Casualties," *Washington Post* (Feb. 20, 2002). On the Third Geneva Convention, see: Geneva Convention (III) Relative to the Treatment of Prisoners of War, 6 U.S.T. 3317, signed on August 12, 1949, at Geneva, Article 17. Although the U.S. has not ratified the Geneva Convention, it has become part of customary international law, and certainly belongs to the war model. Count One of the Lindh indictment charges him with violating 18 U.S.C. 2332(b), "Whoever outside the United States attempts to kill, or engages in a conspiracy to kill, a national of the United States" may be sentenced to 20 years (for attempts) or life imprisonment (for conspiracies). Subsection (c) likewise criminalizes "engag[ing] in physical violence with intent to cause serious bodily injury to a national of the United States; or with the result that serious bodily injury is caused to a national of the United States." Lawful combatants are defined in the Hague Convention (IV) Respecting the Laws and Customs of War on Land, Annex to the Convention, 1 Bevans 631, signed on October 18, 1907, at The Hague, Article 1. The definition requires that combatants "have a fixed distinctive emblem recognizable at a distance." Protocol I Additional to the Geneva Conventions of 1949, 1125 U.N.T.S. 3, adopted on June 8, 1977, at Geneva, Article 44(3) makes an important change in the Hague Convention, expanding the definition of combatants to include non-uniformed irregulars. However, the United States has not agreed to Protocol I. The source of Ruth Wedgwood's remarks: Interview with Melissa Block, National Public Radio program, "All Things Considered" (January 18, 2002); Gary Solis, "Even a 'Bad Man' Has Rights," *Washington Post* (June 25, 2002); *Ex parte Quirin*, 317 U.S. 1, 31 (1942). On the torture of the Pakistani militant by Philippine police: Doug Struck et al., "Borderless Network Of Terror; Bin Laden Followers Reach Across Globe," *Washington Post* (September 23, 2001): "'For weeks, agents hit him with a chair and a long piece of wood, forced water into his mouth, and crushed lighted cigarettes into his private parts,' wrote journalists Marites Vitug and Glenda Gloria in 'Under the Crescent Moon,' an acclaimed book on Abu Sayyaf. 'His ribs were almost totally broken and his captors were surprised he survived.'" On U.S. and Swedish transfers of Isamic militants to countries employing torture: Rajiv Chandrasakaran & Peter Finn, "U.S. Behind Secret Transfer of Terror Suspects," *Washington Post* (March 11, 2002); Peter Finn, "Europeans Tossing Terror Suspects Out the Door," *Washington Post* (January 29, 2002); Anthony Shadid, "Fighting Terror/Atmosphere in Europe, Military Campaign/Asylum Bids; in Shift, Sweden Extradites Militants to Egypt," *Boston Globe* (December 31, 2001). Article 3(1) of the Convention against Torture provides that "No State Party shall expel, return (*'refouler'*) or extradite a person to another State where there are substantial grounds for believing that he would be in danger of being subjected to torture." Article 2(2) cautions that "No exceptional circumstances whatsoever, whether a state of war or a threat of war, internal political instability or any other public emergency, may be invoked as a justification of torture." But no parallel caution is incorporated into Article 3(1)'s non-*refoulement* rule, and a lawyer might well argue that its absence implies that the rule may be abrogated during war or similar public emergency. *Convention against Torture and Other Cruel, Inhuman or Degrading Treatment or Punishment,* 1465 U.N.T.S. 85. Ratified by the United States, Oct. 2, 1994. Entered into force for the United States, Nov. 20, 1994. (Article VI of the U.S. Constitution provides that treaties are the "supreme Law of the Land.")

✎ REVIEW QUESTIONS

1. According to Luban, what is the traditional model of war? What are its four main features? What are its disadvantages?

2. How does Luban describe the law model? How is it combined with the war model to produce a hybrid war-law approach to terrorism?

3. In Luban's view, what is the legal status of al Qaeda suspects? Do they have any rights?

4. Describe the case of the al Qaeda suspects seized in Bosnia.

5. How does Luban explain the concept of enemy combatant? How is this concept applied to Jose Padilla and Yasser Esam Harudi?

6. According to Luban what is the case for the hybrid war-law model? What is the case against it?

7. In Luban's view, what becomes of human rights in the War on Terrorism?

🐝 DISCUSSION QUESTIONS

1. In January 2002, the U.S. military killed 21 innocent civilians in an attack on the Afghani town of Uruzgan. Was this attack justified? Why or why not?
2. Should the Guantanamo prisoners have rights? If so, what are they? If not, why not?
3. Is it acceptable to confine suspected terrorists indefinitely with no trial?
4. Is the hybrid war-law model of the War on Terrorism acceptable? Why or why not?
5. Should torture be used to fight terrorism? Why or why not?

PROBLEM CASES

1. The Draft

According to the U.S. Selective Service System (www.sss.gov), if you are a man ages eighteen to twenty-five, you are legally required to register with the Selective Service System. You can register online or at any U.S. post office.

Congress passed the law requiring registration in 1980, but currently, it is not being enforced. Since 1986, no one has been prosecuted for failure to register, but this could change if the Selective Service starts drafting men—that is, calling men up for mandatory military service. (No one has been drafted since 1973 when conscription ended.) The mission of the Selective Service System is to "serve the emergency manpower needs of the Military by conscripting untrained manpower, or personnel with professional health care skills, if directed by Congress and the President in a national crisis." The national crisis could be the ongoing wars in Iraq and Afghanistan, a war with Iran, or some other conflict.

During the Vietnam War, many young men were drafted to fight in this unpopular war. There were many ways to avoid the draft. One way was to get a college deferment. This was how Dick Cheney and Paul Wolfowitz, the advocates of the Iraq War, avoided military service. President Bill Clinton also had a college deferment. President George W. Bush used his family connections to get in the National Guard, which involved low-risk duty in the United States. Another avoidance tactic was to get a medical rejection by claiming to be suicidal or a homosexual. Men with criminal records were rejected, as well as those saying they were communists. As a last resort, some men went to Canada, which did not support the Vietnam War.

Perhaps the most famous draft resister was boxer Muhammad Ali. In 1967, he refused induction into the armed forces. He maintained that fighting in the Vietnam War was against his Muslim religion and famously said, "I ain't got no quarrel with those Vietcong." He was convicted of refusing induction, sentenced to five years in prison, and not allowed to box professionally for more than three years. In late 1971, the Supreme Court reversed his conviction.

The Iraq War has produced enormous strain in the U.S. voluntary army. Soldiers are suffering from extended and repeated tours of duty. Many soldiers and officers are not re-enlisting. As a result, some leaders are calling for a reinstatement of the draft. U.S. Representative Charles Rangel (D-N.Y.) has argued that poor men and women are far more likely to enlist for military service, and this is unfair. The draft would ensure that the rich and the poor equally share military service in Iraq and other wars. Also, he argues that a country with conscription would be less likely to engage in military adventures like the one in Iraq.

In December 2006, President Bush announced that he was sending more troops to Iraq, and the next day the Selective Service System announced that it was getting ready to test the system's operations. Should the draft be reinstated? Under what circumstances, if any, would you be willing to be drafted? The question applies to women as well as men.

If we draft men for military service, why not draft women too? Other countries such as Israel draft women. Women now serve in the U. S. military with distinction; they fly jets and command troops in combat. There are plenty of young women who are just as capable as young men. Why shouldn't women be drafted?

As we have seen, during the Vietnam War many men avoided the draft by getting a college deferment.

The Selective Service System has modified this rule. Now a deferment lasts only to the end of the semester, or if a man is a senior, he can defer until the end of the academic year. Should there be college deferments? Is this fair?

During the Vietnam War, a man who claimed to be homosexual was not drafted. Currently, the armed forces discharge any person who is openly gay or lesbian. Should gay men or lesbians be drafted? Why or why not?

Why limit the draft to citizens aged eighteen to twenty-five? Why not draft older and younger people too? Is this a good idea? Why or why not?

2. The Iraq War

(For information, books, and articles on the Iraq War, see the Suggested Readings.) After a long buildup, U.S. and British troops invaded Iraq in March 2003. Four years later, 142,000 U.S. troops remained in Iraq fighting sectarian violence; the troops were caught in a civil war being fought by Sunni and Shiite militants.

At least two goals were accomplished by the war: First, Saddam Hussein, the brutal dictator of Iraq, was captured, given a trial, found guilty, and executed. Second, a democratically elected government, led by Prime Minister Nouri al-Maliki, took power in 2006. In 2007, we were waiting to see if the Shiite-dominated government could stop the sectarian violence and unite the country.

The war produced casualties and it was expensive. Nearly 3,500 U.S. troops were killed, and more than 25,000 injured. More than one-half of those injured returned to duty, but about 12,000 have serious injuries such as spinal cord injury or brain damage that will require lifelong treatment. No reliable data exist for Iraqi casualties. One estimate is that the total number of deaths for all Iraqi civilians, military personnel, and insurgents is at least 70,000 and may be as high as 655,000. Another estimate is that 753,209 Iraqi civilians have been killed, and 1,355,776 have been seriously injured. About 2 million people, including many professionals, have left Iraq, and another 2 million have been displaced inside Iraq's borders.

From 2003 to 2007, the war cost the United States about $430 billion. According to Martin Wolk, the chief economics correspondent for MSNBC, the war in 2007 continued to cost more than $200 million a day. He estimates the total economic impact for the United States will be up to $2 trillion.

What was the justification for this war? First, there was the prevention argument. In its most basic form, this is the argument that if one nation threatens another, or might be able to threaten another, then the threatened nation is justified in attacking the nation making the actual or possible threat. The Bush administration claimed that Iraq was possibly a threat to the United States and her allies, and that was the reason for attacking. In the words of President Bush's National Security Statement, the United States must "stop rogue states and their terrorist clients before they are able to threaten or use weapons of mass destruction against the United States and our allies and friends."

One problem with this statement is that Iraq did not have the alleged weapons of mass destruction or the programs to develop them. According to Hans Blix, the head of the UN inspections team, the UN inspections had been effective in eliminating the weapons or the programs to develop them. The Iraq Study Group came to similar conclusions. There was no solid evidence of the existence of the weapons or programs.

Another problem with President Bush's statement is that there was no credible evidence that Saddam Hussein was connected to either the 9/11 attacks or to the al Qaeda organization. Richard A. Clarke, the counterterrorism czar in both the Clinton and Bush administrations, claimed that President Bush was eager to attack Iraq from the beginning of his administration and used the 9/11 attacks as an excuse to link Hussein and al Qaeda in the war on terrorism. Furthermore, it has been claimed that the Muslim terrorists hated the secular government of Saddam Hussein and welcomed its demise. The al Qaeda organization was happy to see Hussein executed; it encouraged the violence in Iraq because it created more militants to fight the United States and her allies.

The main problem with the prevention argument is that it makes it too easy to justify war. Iraq was not an actual threat but might be "able to threaten," and that was enough justification for war, at least according to President Bush's statement. But on just war theory, war should be the last resort, not the first thing considered. Even Henry Kissinger, surely no peacenik, acknowledged this problem when he warned against using the appeal to prevention as a universal principle available to every nation. For example, during the cold war, the USSR was actually threatened by the United States, which had thousands of missiles with nuclear warheads targeting Russian cities and military bases. Even today, the United States has at least 6,000 nuclear warheads, which could be launched in a crisis or because of an accident; also, the United States reserves the right to strike first. The United States is certainly an actual threat to Russia. Does that justify a Russian first strike?

North Korea is a rogue state that has nuclear weapons and may be selling them to other countries. Are we justified in attacking North Korea? (The fact that we have not makes a good case for having nuclear weapons; they are an effective deterrent.) Iran is probably developing nuclear weapons. Should we attack Iran before it is able to produce them? This is not merely a hypothetical question. In May 2007, Vice-President Dick Cheney, standing in front of five F-18 Super Hornet warplanes on a U.S. aircraft carrier, said that the United States was prepared to attack Iran to prevent it from "gaining nuclear weapons."

A second argument used to justify the Iraq War was the humanitarian argument that Saddam Hussein was a brutal dictator, comparable to Hitler, who needed to be removed from power. No doubt Hussein was an evil man, having launched aggressive wars against Iran and Kuwait, gassed thousands of Kurds, killed numerous rivals, and at least attempted to develop chemical, biological, and nuclear weapons before this was stopped by the UN inspections. But this seems to be an argument for assassination, not war. The CIA tried to kill Fidel Castro several times because he was perceived to be evil, but the United States has not launched a massive invasion of Cuba. Why not? (The Bay of Pigs operation was not an all-out military operation with "shock and awe" like the Iraq War.) Besides, like the prevention argument, the humanitarian argument makes it too easy to justify war. Should we go to war against any and all countries ruled by evil men?

A third argument used to justify the war is the legalistic argument that war with Iraq was necessary to enforce the UN resolutions in the face of Iraqi defiance. But France, Germany, and other member nations of the United Nations argued that more inspections would do the job because Iraq was allowing them. And in the event that war was necessary, it should have been undertaken by a genuine coalition of member nations and not just by the United States and Britain with token forces from other nations.

As the bloody occupation continued in 2007, with civilian and military casualties mounting every day, pundits, analysts, and journalists offered various other justifications for war and permanent occupation by U.S. forces. One was the nation-building argument, the view that turning despotic regimes in the Middle East into secular democracies would be a good thing. This view was attributed to former Bush administration officials such as Paul Wolfowitz. However, there was the possibility that Iraq would end up being a fundamentalist Islamic state like Iran. Critics of the war maintained that the real reason for the war was President Bush getting back at his father's enemy. European critics thought the war was really about oil: America wanted to control one of the world's largest oil reserves. They pointed to President Bush's connection to the oil industry and to the fact that Halliburton, the company run by Dick Cheney before he became vice-president, was immediately given the contract to rebuild Iraq's oil industry.

All things considered, was the Iraq War justified or not? Can it be justified using just war theory? Can it be justified in some other way? Explain your position.

3. Jose Padilla

Mr. Padilla, thirty-six, was born in Brooklyn and raised in Chicago. He served prison time for a juvenile murder in Illinois and for gun possession in Florida. He converted to Islam in prison and took the name Abdullah al Muhijir when he lived in Egypt. According to the U.S. government, he also spent time in Saudi Arabia, Pakistan, and Afghanistan.

The FBI arrested Mr. Padilla in May 2002 when he arrived from overseas at Chicago's O'Hare International Airport. Then he was held incommunicado at a Navy brig in Charleston, S.C., for three and one-half years, where he was denied counsel. No formal charges were brought against Mr. Padilla during this time, but not long after his arrest, Attorney General John Ashcroft claimed that Mr. Padilla was part of a plot by al Qaeda to explode a radiological dirty bomb.

On December 18, 2003, a federal appeals court in Manhattan ruled (2 to 1) that the president does not have the executive authority to hold American citizens indefinitely without access to lawyers simply by declaring them to be enemy combatants. The decision said that the president does not have the constitutional authority as Commander in Chief to detain as enemy combatants American citizens seized on American soil, away from the zone of combat. Furthermore, the ruling said, citing a 1971 statute, that Congress did not authorize detention of an American citizen under the circumstances of Mr. Padilla's case. The court ordered the government to release Mr. Padilla from military custody.

On the same day as the court's decision, the Department of Justice issued a statement on the case. The government's statement said that Mr. Padilla was associated with senior al Qaeda leaders including Osama bin Laden and that he had received training from al Qaeda operatives on wiring explosive devices and on the construction of a uranium-enhanced explosive device. The statement concluded that Mr. Padilla "is an enemy combatant who poses a serious and continuing threat to the American people and our national security."

Mr. Padilla appealed his case to the U.S. Supreme Court, but the court declined to take the case because it was moot. In November 2005, as the court challenge to his status was pending, the Bush administration suddenly announced that criminal charges had been filed against him in Miami. He was moved out of military custody to Miami, where he is now being held without bail. Instead of being charged as an enemy combatant, now he is accused of being part of a North American support cell for Islamic extremists. His lawyers have sought to have the charges dismissed on the grounds that the psychological damage he suffered during his long confinement from abuse and extreme isolation have left him incompetent to stand trial. The judge in the case denied the motion; the trial is scheduled for September 9, 2007.

This case raises some troubling questions. Does the government have the legal power to imprison American citizens indefinitely without bringing any charges and denying access to counsel? Is this constitutional? Do citizens charged with a crime have a right to a speedy trial?

In addition to Mr. Padilla, some 600 men of varying nationalities are being held at the Guantanamo Bay naval base in Cuba. These men were captured in Afghanistan and Pakistan during the operations against the Taliban. Like Mr. Padilla, they are deemed by the U.S. government to be enemy combatants having no legal rights. They are not being allowed to contest their detention through petitions for habeas corpus, the ancient writ which for centuries has been used in the English-speaking world to challenge the legality of confinement.

The basic issue is whether or not the president should have the power to deny basic rights in the name of fighting terrorism. What is your view of this?

4. Fighting Terrorism

What can the United States do to prevent terrorist attacks like the September 11 assault on the World Trade Center and the Pentagon? One proposal is national identity cards, discussed by Daniel J. Wakin in *The New York Times,* October 7, 2001. According to polls taken after the attacks, about 70 percent of Americans favor such cards, which are used in other countries. French citizens are required to carry national ID cards, and they may be stopped by the police for card inspection at any time. Such cards are also required in Belgium, Greece, Luxembourg, Portugal, and Spain. Privacy International, a watchdog group in London, estimates that about one hundred countries have compulsory national IDs. Some, like Denmark, issue ID numbers at birth, around which a lifetime of personal information accumulates.

It is not clear if required ID cards would violate the U.S. Constitution. One objection is that a police demand to see the card would constitute a "seizure" forbidden by the Fourth Amendment. Another objection is that illegal immigrants would be targeted rather than terrorists. But proponents of the cards argue that they could be used to identify terrorists and protect travelers. Larry Ellison, the chief executive of the software maker Oracle, claims that people's fingerprints could be embedded on the cards and police or airport guards could scan the cards and check the fingerprints against a database of terrorists. The cards could protect airline travelers at check-in and guard against identity theft. Advocates of the cards argue that there is already a great deal of personal information gathered by private industry, any invasion of privacy caused by the ID cards would not matter much. What do you think? Are national ID cards a good way to fight against terrorism?

Another proposal is to allow suspicionless searches. In Israel, the police can search citizens and their belongings at any time without any particular cause or suspicion. These searches are conducted at shopping centers, airports, stadiums, and other public places. Citizens are also required to pass through metal detectors before entering public places. The U.S. Constitution requires police to have an objective suspicion or "probable cause" to search you, your belongings, or your car, but the Supreme Court has granted exceptions such as border searches and drunk-driving checkpoints. Why not allow suspicionless searches at public places like shopping centers, airports, and football stadiums?

Even more controversial is racial profiling. Israeli authorities single out travelers and citizens for questioning and searches based on racial profiling. Experts cite vigorous racial profiling as one of the reasons Israeli airplanes are not hijacked. The U.S. Supreme Court has not ruled on whether racial profiling violates the equal protection clause of the U.S. Constitution and has declined to hear cases on the practice. Opinions differ on what counts as racial profiling and when or if it is unconstitutional. Advocates of the practice claim that police already practice racial profiling and that it is effective in preventing crime. Critics object that it is nothing more than racism. Is racial profiling justified in the fight against terrorism?

In Canada, police are allowed to arrest and hold suspected terrorists without charges and without bail for up to ninety days. In France, suspects can be held for questioning for nearly five days without being charged and without having any contact with an attorney. Britain's antiterrorist legislation allows suspicious individuals to be detained for up to seven days without a court appearance. The new antiterrorist legislation proposed by the U.S. Congress would allow authorities to hold foreigners suspected of terrorist activity for up to a week without charges. Is this indefinite holding without charges and without bail acceptable?

Finally, in the fight against terrorism Israel has condoned assassinations or "judicially sanctioned executions," that is, killing terrorist leaders such as Osama bin Laden. The United States does not currently permit assassination, but this prohibition stems from an executive order that could be repealed, not because it is forbidden by the Constitution. Should the United States reconsider its position on assassination?

In general, are these methods of fighting terrorism acceptable to you or not? Why or why not?

5. National Missile Defense

National Missile Defense (NMD) is the controversial $8.3-billion missile defense shield championed by President George W. Bush and his Secretary of Defense, Donald Rumsfeld. It is an updated version of President Reagan's Strategic Defense Initiative. More than $60 billion already has been spent on the missile defense program in the last two decades.

The basic idea of NMD is appealing. Instead of ensuring peace by relying on the Cold War strategy of MAD (mutual assured destruction), where neither the United States nor Russia can defend against nuclear attack but can destroy the other if attacked, NMD would protect the United States from missile attack with a defensive umbrella of antimissile missiles. This would give the United States an advantage over Russia or other nuclear powers not having any missile defense.

Russia is no longer seen as the main threat, even though Russia still has thousands of long-range missiles left over from the Cold War arms race. According to President Bush, the main threat to the United States comes from so-called rogue nations unfriendly to the United States such as North Korea and Iraq. In view of the September 11 attacks, the al Qaeda terrorist network of Osama bin Laden also should be considered a threat. Bin Laden has promised more terrorist attacks on the United States and has proclaimed a jihad against the United States. Even though these terrorists do not possess nuclear weapons or missiles at present (or as far as we know, they don't) it seems likely that they will acquire them in the future. Then they could hold America hostage by threatening a nuclear attack or they might launch a surprise attack on an undefended American city such as New York City or Los Angeles.

Even though it seems like a good idea, NMD has problems. There is a good chance that it would not work in an actual attack. Two out of four major missile defense tests conducted so far have failed. Critics say that trying to hit a missile with another missile is like trying to shoot down a bullet with another bullet. It is difficult, to say the least. Countermeasures such as dummy missiles or balloons could fool the defense system. Low-tech missiles, the most likely to be used,

do not go in a predictable path so they would be missed by antimissile missiles.

Even if the defensive system worked perfectly, it would only defend against long-range missiles and not against nuclear weapons delivered by other means. For example, a short-range missile could be launched from a submarine just off the coast, or a weapon could be taken to its target by truck or a private shipper. The most likely scenario is that terrorists would assemble a nuclear weapon at the target and then explode it. Obviously, NMD is no defense against such terrorist attacks.

Finally, there are political problems. NMD violates the 1972 Antiballistic Missile Treaty with Russia. The treaty limits the testing and deployment of new defense systems. Russian President Vladimir Putin contends that violating the 1972 treaty will upset nuclear stability and result in a new arms race.

Given these problems and how much it will cost, is NMD a good idea? What is your position?

6. *Mini-Nukes*

(For more details, see Fred Kaplan, "Low-Yield Nukes," posted November 21, 2003, on http://www.slate.msn.com.)

In 1970, the United States signed the Non-Proliferation Treaty. This Treaty involved a pact between nations having nuclear weapons and nations not having them. Nations not having them promised to not develop nuclear weapons, and nations already having them promised to pursue nuclear disarmament. In 1992 the United States unilaterally stopped nuclear testing, on orders of the first President Bush, and then formalized this in 1995 by signing the Comprehensive Test Ban Treaty. It prohibits the testing and development of nuclear weapons indefinitely, and it was signed by 186 other nations.

In 2003, the second Bush administration insisted that Iran and North Korea halt their nuclear-weapons programs, and argued that the invasion and occupation of Iraq was justified because Iraq had weapons of mass destruction or WMD, that is, chemical, biological, and nuclear weapons (or at least a nuclear weapons program). Yet at the same time, the second Bush administration was actively developing a new generation of exotic nuclear weapons including low-yield mini-nukes and earth-penetrating nukes, despite the

fact that the country already had 7,650 nuclear warheads and bombs. Specifically, the Fiscal Year 2004 defense bill, passed by both houses of Congress in November 2003, did four things. First, it repealed the 1992 law banning the development of low-yield nuclear weapons. Second, the bill provided $15 million to develop an earth-penetrating nuclear weapon, a bunker buster. Third, it allocated $6 million to explore special-effects bombs, for example, the neutron bomb that enhances radiation. Finally, the bill provided $25 million for underground nuclear tests.

This renewed development of nuclear weapons and testing violated the 1970 and 1995 Treaties, but the second Bush administration argued that it was necessary to do this for self-defense. The old warheads mounted on intercontinental missiles were designed to wipe out industrial complexes or destroy whole cities. But such weapons were never used, and it appeared that they had no utility. Certainly they were not effective against suicide bombers or other terrorist attacks. What was needed, it was argued, was smaller warheads that could destroy underground bunkers or WMD storage sites.

Critics argued that the U.S. development of more nuclear weapons undermined the attempt to stop similar development in other nations. If the United States needed nuclear weapons for self-defense, then why didn't other nations need them too? The fact that the United States did not attack North Korea (which had nuclear weapons) seemed to support the view that nations needed these weapons to deter attacks.

Furthermore, critics argued that mini-nukes or bunker busters were not necessary. Conventional weapons could do the job. The United States already had at least two non-nuclear smart bombs that could penetrate the earth before exploding. There was the GBU-24, a 2000-pound laser-guided bomb, and the BLU-109 JDAM, a 2000-pound satellite-guided bomb. Both of these bombs could be filled with incendiary explosive that will burn whatever biological or chemical agents might be stored in an underground site.

So why did the United States need to develop more nuclear weapons? Was this necessary or effective for self-defense? Explain your answer. And why did the United States continue to have 7,650 nuclear warheads and bombs? Was it ever necessary to have so many weapons? Is it necessary now? What is your view?

7. The Gulf War

(For a book-length treatment of the Gulf War, including the view of it as jihad, see Kenneth L. Vaux, *Ethics and the Gulf War* [Boulder, CO: Westview Press, 1992].) In August 1990, the Iraqi army invaded and occupied Kuwait. Although the United States had received warnings, officials did not take them seriously. Saddam Hussein believed the United States would not intervene and apparently had received assurances to that effect. Hussein claimed that the invasion was justified because Kuwait had once been part of Iraq and because the Kuwaitis were exploiting the Rumalla oilfield, which extended into Iraq. The immediate response of the United States and its allies was to begin a ship embargo against Iraq. President George Bush, citing atrocities against the Kuwaitis, compared Hussein to Hitler. For his part, Hussein declared the war to be jihad and threatened the mother of all battles (as he put it) if the Americans dared to intervene. Iran's Ayatollah Khomeini, certainly no friend of the United States, seconded the claim of jihad, adding that anyone killed in battle would be a martyr and immediately go to paradise, the Islamic heaven.

In the months that followed, Iraq ignored repeated ultimatums to leave Kuwait. But Iraq did try to stall for time, following the Koranic teaching of "withholding your hand a little while from war" (Vaux, 1992: 71). Thousands of foreign prisoners were released, and Iraq responded positively to French and Soviet peace initiatives. At the same time, Saddam Hussein continued to call it a holy war, saying that the United States was a satanic force attacking the religious values and practices of Islam.

On January 16, 1991, after a U.N. deadline had passed, the allied forces (American, British, French, Saudi, and Kuwaiti) launched a massive day-and-night air attack on military targets in Iraq, including the capital city of Baghdad. The forty days of air war that followed was very one sided. The allied forces were able to bomb targets at will using advanced technical weapons such as radar-seeking missiles, laser-guided bombs, stealth fighters that avoided radar detection, and smart cruise missiles that could adjust their course. The Iraqi air force never got off the ground, but hid or flew to Iran. The Iraqi Scud missiles killed twenty-two American soldiers sleeping in Saudi Arabia and civilians in Israel but were mostly unreliable and ineffective. Finally, the ground war (Operation Desert Storm) lasted only 100 hours before the allied forces liberated Kuwait City. The Iraqis had more that 200,000 casualties (according to American estimates) while the allied forces sustained less than 200 casualties.

Can this war be justified using the just war theory? Carefully explain your answer. Keep in mind that some religious leaders at the time said that it was not a just war.

Was this really a jihad, as Saddam Hussein and the Ayatollah Khomeini said? Remember that Kuwait and Saudi Arabia are also Muslim countries.

Oil presented another consideration. Kuwait had about 20 percent of the world's known oil reserves at the time. Some said the war was really about the control and price of oil and argued that if Kuwait had not had valuable resources, the United States would not have intervened. (For example, the United States did nothing when China invaded and occupied a defenseless Tibet in 1949.)

8. Gandhi

Gandhi's life is beautifully portrayed in the movie *Gandhi* (1982), directed by Richard Attenborough, with Ben Kingsley as Gandhi. Gandhi's views on war are collected in Madadev Desai, ed., *Nonviolence in Peace and War,* 2 vols. (Ahmedalbad: Navajivan Press, 1945).

Mohandas Gandhi (1869–1948) was the most famous and effective pacifist of the twentieth century. After achieving reforms in the treatment of Hindus and Muslims in South Africa, he returned to India, where he campaigned against British rule, resulting in the departure of the British in 1948, the same year that Gandhi was killed by an orthodox Hindu.

Gandhi was a Hindu who practiced *ahimsa* (nonviolence) toward all living things. (He was considered unorthodox, however, because he rejected the caste system and did not accept everything in the Vedas, the Hindu sacred scriptures.) The concept of ahimsa originated in Jainism and was accepted by both Buddhism and Hinduism. In those religions, ahimsa is understood as not harming any living thing by actions of body, mind, or speech. In Jainism, ahimsa is practiced even with respect to plants, whereas in Hinduism and Buddhism, plants are not included, but nonhuman animals are.

The most original aspect of Gandhi's teaching and methods was what he called *satyagraha* (literally, "truth force"). Satyagraha involves ahimsa and austerities such as fasting. It is supposed to purify one's soul and transform the souls of those it is used against. In practice, the methods of satyagraha developed by Gandhi included marches, demonstrations, sit-ins, strikes, boycotts, fasts, and prayers. These nonviolent and passive methods worked well against the British and have been widely admired and copied. In the United States, Dr. Martin Luther King, Jr. (1929–1968), used similar tactics in the civil rights struggles of the 1950s and 1960s.

Gandhi's nonviolent tactics worked against the British, but would they have been effective against someone like Hitler, who was willing to kill millions of innocent people? Would they stop terrorist attacks such as the September 11 attacks? Is nonviolent resistance an acceptable alternative to war? Is it effective in fighting terrorism? Explain your answers.

✥ SUGGESTED READINGS

For the official Bush administration view of the war on terrorism and the Iraq War, see the CIA website (www.cia.org) and the FBI website (www.fbi.org). For pacifist views, see www.antiwar.com and www.nonviolence.org. The Arab perspective is presented at www.iwpr.net.

Osama bin Laden, "To the Americans," in *Messages to the World,* ed. B. Lawrence (London: Verso, 2005), 162–172. This letter gives bin Laden's reasons for the 9/11 attacks. It was published in the *London Observer* on November 24, 2002. An al Qaeda document that attempts to justify the 9/11 attacks is available in English translation at www.mepc.org.

Hans Blix, *Disarming Iraq* (New York: Pantheon Books, 2004), concludes that every claim made by the Bush administration about Iraq's weapons programs—the mobile biological labs, the yellowcake, the aluminum tubes—has proven to be false and that the Iraq War was unnecessary.

Richard A. Clarke, *Against All Enemies* (New York: Free Press, 2004). Clarke was the counterterrorism coordinator in both the Clinton and the second Bush administrations. He claims that President George W. Bush was obsessed with Iraq after the 9/11 attacks and eager to blame Iraq even though there was overwhelming evidence that al Qaeda was responsible and Saddam Hussein was not.

Christopher Hitchens, *A Long Short War* (London: Plume, 2003), is an enthusiastic supporter of the Iraq War. He claims that it liberated the Iraqis from oppression and prevented Iraq from attacking the United States with nuclear weapons.

Robert Kagan and William Kristol, "The Right War for the Right Reasons," in *The Right War,* ed. Gary Kosen (Cambridge: Cambridge University Press, 2005), 18–35, defend the Iraq War. They claim that Saddam Hussein had "undeniable ties" to terrorists, was a brutal dictator, and was pursuing weapons of mass destruction.

Jan Narveson, "Regime Change," in *A Matter of Principle,* ed. Thomas Cushman (Berkeley: University of California Press, 2005), 58–75, presents the case for regime change in Iraq. He argues that military intervention in Iraq was justified because it produced a decent regime "at modest cost to the

Iraqis" and "at quite modest cost in lives to the Coalition" (p. 74).

C. A. J. Coady, "Terrorism and Innocence," *Journal of Ethics* 8 (2004): 37–58, discusses problems with defining terrorism and deciding who is innocent.

Burleigh Taylor Wilkins, *Terrorism and Collective Responsibility* (London: Routledge, 1992), argues that terrorism can be morally justified in certain circumstances. For example, terrorism aimed at defeating Hitler would have been justified.

Whitley R. P. Kaufman, "Terrorism, Self-Defense, and the Killing of the Innocent," *Social Philosophy Today* 20 (2004): 41–52, argues that terrorism violates the moral prohibition against harming the innocent, and as such, it is always morally impermissible.

Andrew Valls, "Can Terrorism Be Justifed?" in *Ethics in International Affairs,* ed. Andrew Valls (Lanham, MD: Roman & Littlefield, 2000), 65–79, argues that if war can be justified using just war theory, then terrorism can be justified as well.

Virginia Held, "Legitimate Authority in Non-state Groups Using Violence," *Journal of Social Philosophy* 36, 2 (Summer 2005): 175–193, argues that in actual circumstances, such as the struggle to gain independence in South Africa, some uses of violence may be justified, and terrorism may be as justified as war.

Steve Coll, *Ghost Wars* (London: Penguin Press, 2004), explains the history of al Qaeda in Afghanistan, including how Saudi Arabia aided the rise of Osama bin Laden and Islamic extremism.

Ahmed Rashid, *Taliban: Militant Islam, Oil, and Fundamentalism in Central Asia* (New Haven CT: Yale University Press, 2000), presents the history of the Taliban and explains their version of Islam. They believe they are God's invincible soldiers fighting an unending war against unbelievers.

Anthony H. Cordesman, *Terrorism, Asymmetric Warfare, and Weapons of Mass Destruction* (Westport, CT: Praeger, 2001), discusses previous commissions on terrorism, the details of homeland defense, and the risk of chemical and biological attacks.

Yossef Bodansky, *Bin Laden: The Man Who Declared War on America* (New York: Random House, 2001). This book is by a well-known expert on terrorism; it covers bin Laden's life and his pursuit of chemical, biological, and nuclear weapons.

Paul R. Pillar, *Terrorism and U.S. Foreign Policy* (Washington, DC: Brookings Institution, 2001), explains the causes of modern terrorism in countries such as Pakistan and Afghanistan and examines the new war against terrorism.

Peter Partner, *God of Battles: Holy Wars of Christianity and Islam* (Princeton, NJ: Princeton University Press, 1998), explains the doctrines of war in Christianity and Islam.

James Turner Johnson, *Mortality and Contemporary Warfare* (New Haven CT: Yale University Press, 1999), presents the history and development of just war theory and its application in the real world.

Bryan Brophy-Baermann and John A. C. Conybeare, "Retaliating against Terrorism," *American Journal of Political Science* 38, 1 (February 1994): 196–210, argue that retaliation against terrorism produces a temporary deviation in attacks but no long-term effect.

Dilip Hiro, *Holy Wars: The Rise of Islamic Fundamentalism* (London: Routledge, 1989), explains the development of Islamic fundamentalism found today in Iran and Afghanistan, where Islam has emerged as a radical ideology of armed warfare.

Ayatollah Ruhollah Khomeini, "Islam Is Not a Religion of Pacifists," in Holy Terror, ed. Amir Taheri (Bethesda, MD: Adler & Adler, 1987), gives a clear statement of the Islamic doctrine of holy war. According to the Ayatollah Khomeini, Islam says, "Kill all the unbelievers just as they would kill you all!"

R. Peters, "Jihad," in *The Encyclopedia of Religion* (New York: Macmillan, 1989), gives a scholarly account of the Islamic concept of jihad and its application to war.

A. Maalory, *The Crusaders Tthrough Arab Eyes* (New York: Schocken Books, 1985), covers two centuries of hostility and war between Muslim Arabs and Christian Crusaders from the West (called Franks), starting with the fall of Jerusalem in 1099. It is a depressing history of invasion, counterinvasion, massacres, and plunder.

Michael Walzer, *Just and Unjust Wars: A Moral Argument with Historical Illustrations* (New York: Basic Books, 1977), develops and defends just war theory and applies the theory to numerous historical cases, such as the Six-Day War, the Vietnam War, the Korean War, and World War II. He argues that the Vietnam War can be justified as assistance to the legitimate government of South Vietnam.

Robert L. Phillips, *War and Justice* (Norman: University of Oklahoma Press, 1984), defends just war theory. He accepts two principles of the theory, the principle of proportionality and the principle of discrimination. The latter principle, however, in turn rests on the doctrine of double effect, which distinguishes between intending to kill and merely foreseeing that death will occur as an unintended consequence of an action.

James Johnson, *The Just War Tradition and the Restraint of War* (Princeton, NJ: Princeton University Press, 1981), explains the historical development of just war theory from the Middle Ages to the present.

Paul Ramsey, *The Just War: Force and Political Responsibility* (New York: Charles Scribner's Sons, 1968). This book is a collection of articles on just war theory, all written by Ramsey. He is a Christian who defends a version of the theory that has an absolute principle of discrimination against killing noncombatants. Yet having accepted this principle, he goes on to claim that the war in Vietnam was justified though it involved killing many noncombatants.

Paul Christopher, *The Ethics of War and Peace* (Englewood Cliffs, NJ: Prentice Hall, 1994). This textbook covers the just war tradition, the international laws on war, and moral issues such as war crimes; reprisals; and nuclear, biological, and chemical weapons.

Immanuel Kant, *Perpetual Peace* (New York: Liberal Arts Press, 1957). In a classic discussion, Kant maintains that war must not be conducted in a way that rules out future peace. Perpetual peace results when democratic countries let the people decide about going to war. Kant believes that the people will always vote for peace.

Albert Schweitzer, *The Teaching of Reverence for Life,* trans. Richard and Clara Masters (New York: Holt, Rinehart and Winston, 1965), argues that all taking of life is wrong because all life is sacred.

Leo Tolstoy, *The Law of Love and the Law of Violence,* trans. Mary Koutouzow Tolstoy (New York: Holt, Rinehart and Winston, 1971), explains his Christian pacifism.

Mohandas K. Gandhi, "The Practice of Satyagraha," in *Gandhi: Selected Writings,* ed. Ronald Duncan (New York: Harper & Row, 1971), presents his view of nonviolent resistance as an alternative to war.

T. R. Miles, "On the Limits to the Use of Force," *Religious Studies* 20 (1984): 113–120, defends a version of pacifism that is opposed to all war but not to all use of force. This kind of pacifism would require one to refuse to serve in the military but would not rule out serving as a police officer.

William Earle, "In Defense of War," *The Monist* 57, 4 (October 1973): 561–569 attacks pacifism (defined as the principled opposition to all war) and then gives a justification for the morality and rationality of war.

Jan Narveson, "In Defense of Peace," in *Moral Issues,* ed. Jan Narveson (Oxford: Oxford University Press, 1983), 59–71, replies to Earle. He does not defend pacifism; instead, he argues that whenever there is a war, at least one party is morally unjustified.

Jan Narveson, "Morality and Violence: War, Revolution, Terrorism," in *Matters of Life and Death: New Introductory Essays in Moral Philosophy,* ed. Tom Regan (New York: McGraw Hill, 1993), pp. 121–159. In this survey article, Narveson covers many different issues, including the nature and morality of violence, the right of self-defense, pacifism, just war theory, and terrorism.

Richard A. Wasserstrom, ed., *War and Morality* (Belmont, CA: Wadsworth, 1970), is a collection of articles on the morality of war and other issues. Elizabeth Anscombe discusses the doctrine of double effect as it applies to war. Wasserstrom argues that modern wars are very difficult to justify because innocents are inevitably killed.

Jean Bethke Elshtain, *Women and War* (New York: Basic Books, 1987). What is the feminist view of war? According to Elshtain, some feminists are pacifists working for world peace, whereas others want to reject the traditional noncombatant role of women and become warriors. As a result of the second position, the United States now has a higher percentage of women in the military than any other industrialized nation.

Torture

INTRODUCTION

Factual Background

Humans have been torturing each other for a long time. Throughout the ages, the most common method has been beating. The Romans used the cat-of-nine-tails, a whip having nine tips embedded with lead, nails, and glass; it was used to flog people to extract information. The Chinese used bamboo sticks to beat people. During the Spanish Inquisition, torture was used to get confessions or religious conversions. One common method was called the strappado: The hands were bound behind the back, and the victim was suspended until the joints in the arms and shoulders dislocated. Other torture methods included the rack, the iron maiden, the thumbscrew, the boot, and red-hot pincers applied to the toes, ears, nose, or nipples. In modern times, electricity has become one of the most popular and painful tools of torturers. Prisoners are poked with electric cattle prods or have car battery leads attached to their bodies. Stun weapons are used to deliver shocks up to 75,000 volts. Psychological torture is common and includes prolonged solitary confinement, hooding, stress positions, withholding food and water, sleep deprivation, loud noise, bright light, hot and cold temperatures, nakedness, rape and sexual humiliation, mock executions, water boarding, and the use of dogs. Another method is to inject drugs such as sodium pentothal, which depresses the central nervous system and is supposed to make the subject easier to interrogate.

There are international agreements that prohibit torture. The United Nations Universal Declaration of Human Rights, Article 5, says, "No one shall be subjected to torture or cruel, inhuman, or degrading treatment or punishment." The Geneva Convention, Article 3, prohibits "cruel treatment and torture." It also bans "outrages upon personal dignity, in particular, humiliating and degrading treatment." (See the Problem Case.)

American soldiers at Abu Ghraib prison outside Baghdad, Iraq, violated these prohibitions. According to a 2003 report by Major General Antonio M. Taguba, there were numerous instances of "sadistic, blatant, and wanton criminal abuses," including pouring cold water or phosphoric liquid on naked detainees, threatening them with rape or death, sodomizing them with broomsticks, and using military dogs to bite them. There is the well-known picture of a hooded man forced to stand on a box with wires attached to his hands and neck. Reportedly, he was told that he would be electrocuted if he stepped or fell off the box. Former prisoners tell stories of U.S. soldiers beating prisoners, sometimes to death. Mohammed Unis Hassan says that he was cuffed to bars of his cell and then a female soldier poked his eye with her fingers so hard that he couldn't see afterward. Now his left eye is gray and glassy and his vision blurred. He says he saw an old man forced to lie naked on his face until he died. Other naked prisoners were threatened and bitten by attack dogs.

Some of the mistreatment at Abu Ghraib involved sexual humiliation. There are photographs of naked Iraqi prisoners forced to simulate oral or anal sex. Private Lynndie England is shown giving a thumbs-up sign and pointing to the genitals of a naked and hooded Iraqi as he masturbates. In another picture, Private England is shown with Specialist Charles A. Graner, both grinning and giving the thumbs-up sign in front of a pile of naked Iraqis. Another picture shows Private England leading a naked man around on a dog leash.

Another place where prisoners have been tortured is the U.S. naval base at Guantanamo Bay, Cuba. FBI agents, Red Cross inspectors, and numerous released detainees have alleged that prisoners were chained in a fetal position on the floor or in a baseball catcher's position, subjected to extremes of temperature, made to walk on broken glass or barbed wire, subjected to loud music and flashing lights, given electrical shocks, chained and hanged from the ceiling, and beaten. One of the more bizarre acts was throwing the Quran in the toilet.

The revelation of torture at Abu Ghraib and Guantanamo Bay produced outrage among human rights activists. The response of the Bush administration was a Justice Department memo in 2002 asserting that inflicting moderate pain is not torture. According to the memo, mistreatment is torture only if it produces suffering "equivalent in intensity to the pain accompanying serious physical injury, such as organ failure, impairment of bodily function, or even death." On his talk show, Rush Limbaugh said that the sexual humiliation at Abu Ghraib was just harmless fun, similar to what goes on in college fraternities or secret societies.

In 2006, President Bush signed the McCain Detainee Amendment into law. It prohibits "cruel, inhuman or degrading" treatment of prisoners by U.S. officials or agents. But it is not clear what torture methods are prohibited. The amendment requires that military interrogations follow the U.S. Army's Field Manual on Interrogation, but this document is being rewritten and the section on interrogation techniques is classified. The McCain amendment authorizes any method on the highly classified list of techniques, no matter what they are.

The interrogation methods used by the United States are secret, and they have also been outsourced to other countries. The CIA has been operating covert prisons in eight countries, including Egypt, Thailand, Afghanistan, and several democracies in Eastern Europe. The existence and locations of these facilities, called "black sites," had been classified, but President Bush revealed their existence in September 2006.

He said in a speech that fourteen prisoners had been moved from the CIA's secret prisons in Europe to Guantanamo Bay. The prisoners included Khalid Sheik Mohammed, who confessed to planning the 9/11 attacks. (See the Problem Case.) President Bush said the fourteen prisoners were the last ones remaining in CIA custody, but Manfred Nowak, the UN special investigator on torture, said, "Of course there are many others." In his speech, President Bush said, "The United States does not torture," but he refused to say what specific methods had been used to get confessions from the prisoners.

The Readings

Henry Shue explains why, in his view, torture is morally worse than just-combat killing. Unlike killing in a just war, which supposedly involves a fair fight with winners and losers, torture is not fair and violates the basic moral prohibition against assault on the defenseless. Shue believes this explains in part the peculiar disgust that torture evokes, a disgust not aroused by just-combat killing. Nevertheless, he thinks it cannot be denied that there are imaginable cases where torture might be permissible. These are rare cases where the harm that could be prevented by interrogational torture is so great that it outweighs the cruelty of the torture and the damage done by violating the moral prohibition of torture. The specific example he gives involves a fanatic who has set a hidden nuclear device in the heart of Paris. The only way to prevent disaster in the case is to torture the fanatic to find out where the device is located so that it can be found and deactivated.

David Luban argues that the ticking-bomb story (as he calls Shue's imaginary example) is an intellectual fraud. It paints an unrealistic picture that tricks us into thinking that torture can be justified and that the torturer is not a sadistic brute but a heroic public servant trying to save innocent lives. Luban claims the story cheats by assuming too much—that officials know there is a bomb, that they have captured the one who planted it, that torture will make him talk, and so on. None of this is certain in the real world. Also, the story assumes it is rational to choose between the certainty of torture versus the uncertainty of saving lives and that a decision can be made by calculating costs and benefits. All this is so remote from the real world that the wise course is to deny the possibility. It is a waste of time, insane, or frivolous to try to make a moral decision in this case. Besides, back in the real world, once it is granted that torture is permitted in the imaginary tick-bombing case, we end up with a torture culture with torture practices, training, and institutions.

Heather MacDonald attacks the torture narrative that claims the U.S. government's decision to deny the Geneva Conventions for enemy combatants resulted in torture at Guantanamo and Abu Ghraib. She claims this story is based on ignorance of the actual interrogation techniques used by the military, which are light years away from real torture and controlled by bureaucratic safeguards. The illegal acts at Abu Ghraib were caused by the anarchy of war and not by any official decisions. The interrogation techniques used at Guantanamo are not torture in her view. They are merely stress techniques that include isolation, sleep deprivation, loud noise, prolonged standing, poking, grabbing, and so on. She admits that water boarding of Khalid Sheik Mohammad (see the Problem Case) arguably crosses the line into torture, and she notes that the CIA's behavior remains a "black box." She concludes that to succeed in the war on terrorism, interrogators must be allowed to use these stress techniques on terrorists.

Philosophical Issues

What is torture? There is disagreement about how to define torture and what treatment is considered torture. MacDonald quotes the 2002 memo by Assistant Attorney General Jay S. Bybee, which interprets the 1984 Convention Against Torture as forbidding only physical pain equivalent to that "accompanying serious physical injury, such as organ failure, impairment of bodily function or even death," or mental pain resulting in "significant psychological harm of significant duration, e.g., lasting for months or even years." Following Luban, we can call this "torture heavy."

Techniques such as water boarding, nudity, starvation, or beating would not count as torture heavy if they do not cause serious physical injury or significant psychological harm. They can be called "torture lite," to use Luban's term. Prolonged standing or kneeling, sleep deprivation, and loud noise can be classified as abuse, not torture.

By contrast, The Human Rights Watch statement (also quoted by MacDonald) includes among the effects of torture "long-term depression, post-traumatic stress disorder, marked sleep disturbances and alterations in self-perceptions, not to mention feelings of powerlessness, of fear, guilt and shame." If those are the effects of torture, then all the stress techniques described by MacDonald, and certainly the techniques used by the CIA (see the Problem Case), would count as torture.

What techniques should be allowed when interrogating terrorists? MacDonald's position is that stress techniques including abuse and torture lite should be permitted but not torture heavy, which is the only thing that counts as torture in her view. The Human Rights Watch view is that prisoners should not be tortured, and torture includes not only torture lite and torture heavy but also abuse. Luban agrees that we ought to prohibit abuse. He argues that if we don't prohibit abuse, then it will turn into torture lite, which will turn into torture heavy. In other words, there is a slippery slope where abuse slides into torture. To avoid the slippery slope, we need to draw a bright line at abuse.

Is torture morally wrong? Shue argues that torture is morally worse than killing in a just war; it violates the basic moral prohibition against assault upon the defenseless. Luban says that reverence for human rights and dignity makes torture morally unacceptable. Given these views, both would agree that sadistic torture—that is, torture done merely to cause suffering—is obviously wrong, even if the torturer enjoys it. (Kant famously gave sadistic torture as a counterexample to utilitarianism.) They would agree that torture done to punish a criminal is wrong as well. For one thing, it violates the Eighth Amendment prohibition of cruel and unusual punishment. They would condemn torturing a prisoner to produce a confession. Besides being cruel, torturing to produce a confession is worthless because people will confess to anything under torture. (See the book by William Sampson in the Suggested Readings.) Terroristic torture done to intimidate individuals other than the victim of torture is condemned by Shue as a violation of Kant's principle that no person may be used as only a means.

The debate about the morality of torture in the readings centers around interrogational torture and, specifically, whether torture is morally permitted in a ticking-bomb case. Shue argues that it is, but he expresses some reservations. It has to be a case just like the one he describes, and even if torture is permitted in a rare case, this does not mean that it should be legalized. All torture should remain illegal. Luban does not agree that torture is morally permissible. He argues against allowing torture even in the ticking-bomb case, which he characterizes as a fraud, a picture that bewitches us. His position is that torture, including abuse, should be absolutely prohibited. MacDonald defends the interrogational techniques used by the army; they are not torture, and they must be used if we are going to win the war against terrorism. She does not discuss the ticking-bomb case, and it is safe to assume that she would approve of torture if it resulted in saving thousands of lives.

Torture

HENRY SHUE

Henry Shue is professor of ethics and public life at Cornell University. He is the author of *Basic Rights* (2nd ed., 1980) and many articles on topics in ethics.

Shue argues that torture is morally worse that just-combat killing because it violates the prohibition against assault of the defenseless and the constraint of being a fair fight. This partly explains why torture evokes a peculiar disgust. He goes on to distinguish between terroristic torture, where the torture is used to intimidate others, and interrogational torture, which is used to get information. Terroristic torture does not allow compliance; it is a pure case of violating Kant's principle that no person may be used as a means only, and for that reason, it is wrong. Interrogational torture does allow possible compliance and the possibility of escape, provided the torturers are persuaded that the victim has told all there is to tell and they are willing to stop. Shue suggests there is at least one imaginable case where interrogational torture might be permissible: the case of the fanatic who has hidden a nuclear device set to explode in Paris. In that case, the only way to prevent the destruction of the city is to torture the perpetrator to find out where the device is hidden so that it can be found and deactivated.

But no one dies in the right place
Or in the right hour
And everyone dies sooner than his time
And before he reaches home.

—REZA BARAHENI

Whatever one might have to say about torture, there appear to be moral reasons for not saying it. Obviously I am not persuaded by these reasons, but they deserve some mention. Mostly, they add up to a sort of Pandora's box objection: if practically everyone is opposed to all torture, why bring it up, start people thinking about it,

and risk weakening the inhibitions against what is clearly a terrible business?

Torture is indeed contrary to every relevant international law, including the laws of war. No other practice except slavery is so universally and unanimously condemned in law and human convention. Yet, unlike slavery, which is still most definitely practiced but affects relatively few people, torture is widespread and growing. According to Amnesty International, scores of governments are now using some torture—including governments which are widely viewed as fairly civilized—and a number of governments

Source: "Torture" by Henry Shue from *Philosophy & Public Affairs*, Vol. 7, No. 2, 1977. Reprinted by permission of Blackwell Publishing, Ltd.

are heavily dependent upon torture for their very survival.[1]

So, to cut discussion of this objection short, Pandora's box is open. Although virtually everyone continues ritualistically to condemn all torture publicly, the deep conviction, as reflected in actual policy, is in many cases not behind the strong language. In addition, partial justifications for some of the torture continue to circulate.[2]

One of the general contentions that keeps coming to the surface is: since killing is worse than torture, and killing is sometimes permitted, especially in war, we ought sometimes to permit torture, especially when the situation consists of a protracted, if undeclared, war between a government and its enemies. I shall try first to show the weakness of this argument. To establish that one argument for permitting some torture is unsuccessful is, of course, not to establish that no torture is to be permitted. But in the remainder of the essay I shall also try to show, far more interestingly, that a comparison between some types of killing in combat and some types of torture actually provides an insight into an important respect in which much torture is morally worse. This respect is the degree of satisfaction of the primitive moral prohibition against assault upon the defenseless. Comprehending how torture violates this prohibition helps to explain—and justify—the peculiar disgust which torture normally arouses.

The general idea of the defense of at least some torture can be explained more fully, using "just-combat killing" to refer to killing done in accord with all relevant requirements for the conduct of warfare.[3] The defense has two stages.

A Since (1) just-combat killing is total destruction of a person,
     (2) torture is—usually—only partial destruction or temporary incapacitation of a person, and
     (3) the total destruction of a person is a greater harm than the partial destruction of a person is,
then (4) just-combat killing is a greater harm than torture usually is;
B since (4) just-combat killing is a greater harm than torture usually is, and

     (5) just-combat killing is sometimes morally permissible,
then (6) torture is sometimes morally permissible.

To state the argument one step at a time is to reveal its main weakness. Stage B tacitly assumes that if a greater harm is sometimes permissible, then a lesser harm is too, at least sometimes. The mistake is to assume that the only consideration relevant to moral permissibility is the amount of harm done. Even if one grants that killing someone in combat is doing him or her a greater harm than torturing him or her (Stage A), it by no means follows that there could not be a justification for the greater harm that was not applicable to the lesser harm. Specifically, it would matter if some killing could satisfy other moral constraints (besides the constraint of minimizing harm) which no torture could satisfy.[4]

A defender of at least some torture could, however, readily modify the last step of the argument to deal with the point that one cannot simply weigh amounts of "harm" against each other but must consider other relevant standards as well by adding a final qualification:

     (6′) torture is sometimes morally permissible, provided that it meets whichever standards are satisfied by just-combat killing.

If we do not challenge the judgment that just-combat killing is a greater harm than torture usually is, the question to raise is: Can torture meet the standards satisfied by just-combat killing? If so, that might be one reason in favor of allowing such torture. If not, torture will have been reaffirmed to be an activity of an extremely low moral order.

ASSAULT UPON THE DEFENSELESS

The laws of war include an elaborate, and for the most part long-established, code for what might be described as the proper conduct of the killing of other people. Like most codes, the laws of war have been constructed piecemeal and different bits of the code serve different functions.[5]

It would almost certainly be impossible to specify any one unifying purpose served by the laws of warfare as a whole. Surely major portions of the law serve to keep warfare within one sort of principle of efficiency by requiring that the minimum destruction necessary to the attainment of legitimate objectives be used.

However, not all the basic principles incorporated in the laws of war could be justified as serving the purpose of minimizing destruction. One of the most basic principles for the conduct of war (*jus in bello*) rests on the distinction between combatants and noncombatants and requires that insofar as possible, violence not be directed at noncombatants.[6] Now, obviously, there are some conceptual difficulties in trying to separate combatants and noncombatants in some guerrilla warfare and even sometimes in modern conventional warfare among industrial societies. This difficulty is a two-edged sword; it can be used to argue that it is increasingly impossible for war to be fought justly as readily as it can be used to argue that the distinction between combatants and noncombatants is obsolete. In any case, I do not now want to defend or criticize the principle of avoiding attack upon noncombatants but to isolate one of the more general moral principles this specific principle of warfare serves.

It might be thought to serve, for example, a sort of efficiency principle in that it helps to minimize human casualties and suffering. Normally, the armed forces of the opposing nations constitute only a fraction of the respective total populations. If the casualties can be restricted to these official fighters, perhaps total casualties and suffering will be smaller than they would be if human targets were unrestricted.

But this justification for the principle of not attacking noncombatants does not ring true. Unless one is determined a priori to explain everything in terms of minimizing numbers of casualties, there is little reason to believe that this principle actually functions primarily to restrict the number of casualties rather than, as its own terms suggest, the *types* of casualties.[7] A more convincing suggestion about the best justification which could be given is that the principle goes some way toward keeping combat humane, by protecting those who are assumed to be incapable of defending themselves. The principle of warfare is an instance of a more general moral principle which prohibits assaults upon the defenseless.[8]

Nonpacifists who have refined the international code for the conduct of warfare have not necessarily viewed the killing involved in war as in itself any less terrible than pacifists view it. One fundamental function of the distinction between combatants and noncombatants is to try to make a terrible combat fair, and the killing involved can seem morally tolerable to nonpacifists in large part because it is the outcome of what is conceived as a fair procedure. To the extent that the distinction between combatants and noncombatants is observed, those who are killed will be those who were directly engaged in trying to kill their killers. The fairness may be perceived to lie in this fact: that those who are killed had a reasonable chance to survive by killing instead. It was kill or be killed for both parties, and each had his or her opportunity to survive. No doubt the opportunities may not have been anywhere near equal—it would be impossible to restrict wars to equally matched opponents. But at least none of the parties to the combat were defenseless.

Now this obviously invokes a simplified, if not romanticized, portrait of warfare. And at least some aspects of the laws of warfare can legitimately be criticized for relying too heavily for their justification on a core notion that modern warfare retains aspects of a knightly joust, or a duel, which have long since vanished, if ever they were present. But the point now is not to attack or defend the efficacy of the principle of warfare that combat is more acceptable morally if restricted to official combatants, but to notice one of its moral bases, which, I am suggesting, is that it allows for a "fair fight" by means of protecting the utterly defenseless from assault. The resulting picture of war—accurate or not—is not of victim and perpetrator (or, of mutual victims) but of a winner and a loser, each of whom might have enjoyed, or suffered, the fate of the other. Of course, the satisfaction of the requirement of providing for a "fair fight" would not by itself make a conflict morally acceptable overall. An unprovoked and otherwise unjustified invasion does not become morally acceptable just because attacks upon noncombatants, use of prohibited weapons, and so on are avoided.

At least part of the peculiar disgust which torture evokes may be derived from its apparent failure to satisfy even this weak constraint of being a "fair fight." The supreme reason, of course, is that torture begins only after the fight is—for the victim—finished. Only losers are tortured. A "fair fight" may even in fact already have occurred and led to the capture of the person who is to be tortured. But now that the torture victim has exhausted all means of defense and is powerless before the victors, a fresh assault begins. The surrender is followed by new attacks upon the defeated by the now unrestrained conquerors. In this respect torture is indeed not analogous to the killing in battle of a healthy and well-armed foe; it is a cruel assault upon the defenseless. In combat the other person one kills is still a threat when killed and is killed in part for the sake of one's own survival. The torturer inflicts pain and damage upon another person who, by virtue of now being within his or her power, is no longer a threat and is entirely at the torturer's mercy.

It is in this respect of violating the prohibition against assault upon the defenseless, then, that the manner in which torture is conducted is morally more reprehensible than the manner in which killing would occur if the laws of war were honored. In this respect torture sinks below even the well-regulated mutual slaughter of a justly fought war.

TORTURE WITHIN CONSTRAINTS?

But is all torture indeed an assault upon the defenseless? For, it could be argued in support of some torture that in many cases there is something beyond the initial surrender which the torturer wants from the victim and that in such cases the victim could comply and provide the torturer with whatever is wanted. To refuse to comply with the further demand would then be to maintain a second line of defense. The victim would, in a sense, not have surrendered—at least not

fully surrendered—but instead only retreated. The victim is not, on this view, utterly helpless in the face of unrestrainable assault as long as he or she holds in reserve an act of compliance which would satisfy the torturer and bring the torture to an end.

It might be proposed, then, that there could be at least one type of morally less unacceptable torture. Obviously the torture victim must remain defenseless in the literal sense, because it cannot be expected that his or her captors would provide means of defense against themselves. But an alternative to a capability for a literal defense is an effective capability for surrender, that is, a form of surrender which will in fact bring an end to attacks. In the case of torture the relevant from of surrender might seem to be a compliance with the wishes of the torturer that provides an escape from further torture.

Accordingly, the constraint on the torture that would, on this view, make it less objectionable would be this: the victim of torture must have available an act of compliance which, if performed, will end the torture. In other words, the purpose of the torture must be known to the victim, the purpose must be the performance of some action within the victim's power to perform, and the victim's performance of the desired action must produce the permanent cessation of the torture. I shall refer to torture that provides for such an act of compliance as torture that satisfies the constraint of possible compliance. As soon becomes clear, it makes a great difference what kind of act is presented as the act of compliance. And a person with an iron will, a great sense of honor, or an overwhelming commitment to a cause may choose not to accept voluntarily cessation of the torture on the terms offered. But the basic point would be merely that there should be some terms understood so that the victim retains one last portion of control over his or her fate. Escape is not defense, but it is a manner of protecting oneself. A practice of torture that allows for escape through compliance might seem immune to the charge of engaging in assault upon the defenseless. Such is the proposal.

One type of contemporary torture, however, is clearly incapable of satisfying the constraint of possible compliance. The extraction of information from the victim, which perhaps—whatever the deepest motivations of torturers may have been—has historically been a dominant explicit purpose of torture is now, in world practice, overshadowed by the goal of the intimidation of people other than the victim.[9]... The function of general intimidation of others, or deterrence of dissent, is radically different from the function of extracting specific information under the control of the victim of torture, in respects which are central to the assessment of such torture. This is naturally not to deny that any given instance of torture may serve, to varying degrees, both purposes—and, indeed, other purposes still.

Terroristic torture, as we may call this dominant type, cannot satisfy the constraint of possible compliance, because its purpose (intimidation of persons other than the victim of the torture) cannot be accomplished and may not even be capable of being influenced by the victim of the torture. The victim's suffering—indeed, the victim—is being used entirely as a means to an end over which the victim has no control. Terroristic torture is a pure case—the purest possible case—of the violation of the Kantian principle that no person may be used *only* as a means...

The degree of need for assaults upon the defenseless initially appears to be quite different in the case of torture for the purpose of extracting information, which we may call *interrogational torture.*[10] This type of torture needs separate examination because, however condemnable we ought in the end to consider it overall, its purpose of gaining information appears to be consistent with the observation of some constraint on the part of any torturer genuinely pursuing that purpose alone. Interrogational torture does have a built-in end-point: when the information has been obtained, the torture has accomplished its purpose and need not be continued. Thus, satisfaction of the constraint of possible compliance seems to be quite compatible with the explicit end of interrogational torture, which could be terminated upon the victim's compliance in providing the information sought. In a fairly obvious fashion the torturer could consider himself or herself to have completed the assigned task—or

probably more hopefully, any superiors who were supervising the process at some emotional distance could consider the task to be finished and put a stop to it. A pure case of interrogational torture, then, appears able to satisfy the constraint of possible compliance, since it offers an escape, in the form of providing the information wanted by the torturers, which affords some protection against further assault.

Two kinds of difficulties arise for the suggestion that even largely interrogational torture could escape the charge that it includes assaults upon the defenseless. It is hardly necessary to point out that very few actual instances of torture are likely to fall entirely within the category of interrogational torture. Torture intended primarily to obtain information is by no means always in practice held to some minimum necessary amount. To the extent that the torturer's motivation is sadistic or otherwise brutal, he or she will be strongly inclined to exceed any rational calculations about what is sufficient for the stated purpose. In view of the strength and nature of a torturer's likely passions—of, for example, hate and self-hate, disgust and self-disgust, horror and fascination, subservience toward superiors and aggression toward victims—no constraint is to be counted upon in practice.

Still, it is of at least theoretical interest to ask whether torturers with a genuine will to do so could conduct interrogational torture in a manner which would satisfy the constraint of possible compliance. In order to tell, it is essential to grasp specifically what compliance would normally involve. Almost all torture is "political" in the sense that it is inflicted by the government in power upon people who are, seem to be, or might be opposed to the government. Some torture is also inflicted by opponents of a government upon people who are, seem to be, or might be supporting the government. Possible victims of torture fall into three broad categories: the ready collaborator, the innocent bystander, and the dedicated enemy.

First, the torturers may happen upon someone who is involved with the other side but is not dedicated to such a degree that cooperation with the torturers would, from the victim's perspective, constitute a betrayal of anything highly valued. For such a person a betrayal of cause and allies might indeed serve as a form of genuine escape.

The second possibility is the capture of someone who is passive toward both sides and essentially uninvolved. If such a bystander should happen to know the relevant information—which is very unlikely—and to be willing to provide it, no torture would be called for. But what if the victim would be perfectly willing to provide the information sought in order to escape the torture but does not have the information? ... The victim has no convincing way of demonstrating that he or she cannot comply, even when compliance is impossible. (Compare the reputed dunking test for witches: if the woman sank, she was an ordinary mortal.)

Even a torturer who would be willing to stop after learning all that could be learned, which is nothing at all if the "wrong" person is being tortured, would have difficulty discriminating among pleas. Any keeping of the tacit bargain to stop when compliance has been as complete as possible would likely be undercut by uncertainty about when the fullest possible compliance had occurred...

Finally, when the torturers succeed in torturing someone genuinely committed to the other side, compliance means, in a word, betrayal; betrayal of one's ideals and one's comrades. The possibility of betrayal cannot be counted as an escape. Undoubtedly some ideals are vicious and some friends are partners in crime—this can be true of either the government, the opposition, or both. Nevertheless, a betrayal is no escape for a dedicated member of either a government or its opposition, who cannot collaborate without denying his or her highest values.[11]

For any genuine escape must be something better than settling for the lesser of two evils. One can always try to minimize one's losses—even in dilemmas from which there is no real escape. But if accepting the lesser of two evils always counted as an escape, there would be no situations from which there was no escape, except perhaps those in which all alternatives happened to be equally evil. On such a loose notion of escape, all conscripts would become

volunteers, since they could always desert. And all assaults containing any alternatives would then be acceptable. An alternative which is legitimately to count as an escape must not only be preferable but also itself satisfy some minimum standard of moral acceptability. A denial of one's self does not count.

Therefore, on the whole, the apparent possibility of escape through compliance tends to melt away upon examination. The ready collaborator and the innocent bystander have some hope of an acceptable escape, but only provided that the torturers both (1) are persuaded that the victim has kept his or her part of the bargain by telling all there is to tell and (2) choose to keep their side of the bargain in a situation in which agreements cannot be enforced upon them and they have nothing to lose by continuing the torture if they please. If one is treated as if one is a dedicated enemy, as seems likely to be the standard procedure, the fact that one actually belongs in another category has no effect. On the other hand, the dedicated enemies of the torturers, who presumably tend to know more and consequently are the primary intended targets of the torture, are provided with nothing which can be considered an escape and can only protect themselves, as torture victims always have, by pretending to be collaborators or innocents, and thereby imperiling the members of these two categories.

MORALLY PERMISSIBLE TORTURE?

Still, it must reluctantly be admitted that the avoidance of assaults upon the defenseless is not the only, or even in all cases an overriding, moral consideration. And, therefore, even if terroristic and interrogational torture, each in its own way, is bound to involve attacks upon people unable to defend themselves or to escape, it is still not utterly inconceivable that instances of one or the other type of torture might sometimes, all things considered, be justified....

It cannot be denied that there are imaginable cases in which the harm that could be prevented by a rare instance of pure interrogational torture would be so enormous as to outweigh the cruelty of the torture itself and, possibly, the enormous potential harm which would result if what was intended to be a rare instance was actually the breaching of the dam which would lead to a torrent of torture. There is a standard philosopher's example which someone always invokes: suppose a fanatic, perfectly willing to die rather than collaborate in the thwarting of his own scheme, has set a hidden nuclear device to explode in the heart of Paris. There is no time to evacuate the innocent people or even the movable art treasures—the only hope of preventing tragedy is to torture the perpetrator, find the device, and deactivate it.

I can see no way to deny the permissibility of torture in a case *just like this*. To allow the destruction of much of a great city and many of its people would be almost as wicked as purposely to destroy it, as the Nazis did to London and Warsaw, and the Allies did to Dresden and Tokyo, during World War II. But there is a saying in jurisprudence that hard cases make bad law, and there might well be one in philosophy that artificial cases make bad ethics. If the example is made sufficiently extraordinary, the conclusion that the torture is permissible is secure. But one cannot easily draw conclusions for ordinary cases from extraordinary ones, and as the situations described become more likely, the conclusion that the torture is permissible becomes more debatable.

Notice how unlike the circumstances of an actual choice about torture the philosopher's example is. The proposed victim of our torture is not someone we suspect of planting the device: he *is* the perpetrator. He is not some pitiful psychotic making one last play for attention: he *did* plant the device. The wiring is not backwards, the mechanism is not jammed: the device *will* destroy the city if not deactivated.

Much more important from the perspective of whether general conclusions applicable to ordinary cases can be drawn are the background conditions that tend to be assumed. The torture will not be conducted in the basement of a small-town jail in the provinces by local thugs popping pills; the prime minister and chief justice are being kept informed; and a priest and a doctor are present. The victim will not be raped or forced to eat excrement and will not collapse with a heart attack or become deranged before talking; while avoiding irreparable damage, the antiseptic pain will carefully be increased only up to the point at which the necessary information is divulged, and the doctor will then immediately administer an antibiotic and a tranquilizer. The torture is purely interrogational.[12]

Most important, such incidents do not continue to happen. There are not so many people with grievances against this government that the torture is becoming necessary more often, and in the smaller cities, and for slightly lesser threats, and with a little less care, and so on. Any judgment that torture could be sanctioned in an isolated case without seriously weakening existing inhibitions against the more general use of torture rests on empirical hypotheses about the psychology and politics of torture. There *is* considerable evidence of all torture's metastatic tendency. If there is also evidence that interrogational torture can sometimes be used with the surgical precision which imagined justifiable cases always assume, such rare uses would have to be considered.

Does the possibility that torture might be justifiable in some of the rarefied situations which can be imagined provide any reason to consider relaxing the legal prohibitions against it? Absolutely not. The distance between the situations which must be concocted in order to have a plausible case of morally permissible torture and the situations which actually occur is, if anything, further reason why the existing prohibitions against torture should remain and should be strengthened by making torture an international crime. An act of torture ought to remain illegal so that anyone who sincerely believes such an act to be the least available evil is placed in the position of needing to justify his or her act morally in order to defend himself or herself legally. The torturer should be in roughly the same position as someone who commits civil disobedience. Anyone who thinks an act of torture is justified should have no alternative but to convince a group of peers in a public trial that all necessary conditions for a morally permissible act were indeed satisfied. If it is reasonable to put someone through torture, it is reasonable to put someone else through a careful explanation of why. If the situation approximates those in the imaginary examples in which torture seems possible to justify, a judge can surely be expected to suspend the sentence. Meanwhile, there is little need to be concerned about possible injustice to justified torturers and great need to find means to restrain totally unjustified torture.

NOTES

The time and facilities for this study were provided by the Center for Philosophy and Public Policy of the University of Maryland. For careful critiques of earlier versions I am also grateful to Michael Gardner, Robert Goodin, Ernest Schlaretzki, and especially Peter G. Brown and the editors of *Philosophy & Public Affairs*.

1. See Amnesty International, *Report on Torture* (New York: Farrar, Straus and Giroux, 1975), 21–33.

2. I primarily have in mind conversations which cannot be cited, but for a written source see Roger Trinquier, *La Guerre Moderne* (Paris: La Table Ronde, 1961), 39, 42, 187–191. Consider the following: "Et c'est tricher que d'admettre sereinement que l'artillerie ou l'aviation peuvent bombarder des villages où se trouvent des femmes et des enfants qui seront inutilement massacrés, alors que le plus souvent les ennemis visés auront pu s'enfuir, et refuser que des spécialistes en interrogeant un terroriste permettent de se saisir des vrais coupables et d'épargner les innocents" (42).

3. By "just combat" I mean warfare which satisfies what has traditionally been called *jus in bello*, the law governing how war may be fought once underway, rather than *jus ad bellum*, the law governing when war may be undertaken.

4. Obviously one could also challenge other elements of the argument—most notably, perhaps, premise (3). Torture is usually humiliating and degrading—the pain is normally experienced naked and amidst filth. But while killing destroys life, it need not destroy dignity. Which is worse, an honorable death or a degraded existence? While I am not unsympathetic with this line of attack, I do not want to try to use it. It suffers from being an attempt somehow just to intuit the relative degrees of evil attached respectively to death and degradation. Such judgments should probably be the outcome, rather than the starting point, of an argument. The rest of the essay bears directly on them.

5. See James T. Johnson, *Ideology, Reason, and the Limitation of War: Religious and Secular Concepts 1200–1740* (Princeton: Princeton University Press, 1975). Johnson stresses the largely religious origins of *jus ad bellum* and the largely secular origins of *jus in bello*.

6. For the current law, see Geneva Convention Relative to the Protection of Civilian Persons in Time of War, 12 August 1949 [1955], 6 U.S.T. 3516; T.I.A.S. No. 3365; 75 U.N.T.S. 287. Also see United States, Department of the Army, *The Law of Land Warfare*, Field Manual 27–10 (Washington, DC: Government Printing Office, 1956), chap. 5, "Civilian Persons"; and United States, Department of the Air Force, *International Law—The Conduct of Armed Conflict and Air Operations*, Air Force Pamphlet 110–31 (Washington, DC: Government Printing Office, 1976), chap. 3, "Combatants, Noncombatants and Civilians."

7. This judgment is supported by Stockholm International Peace Research Institute, *The Law of War and Dubious Weapons* (Stockholm: Almqvist and Wiksell, 1976), 9: "The prohibition on deliberately attacking the civilian population as such is not based exclusively on the principle of avoiding unnecessary suffering."

8. To defend the bombing of cities in World War II on the ground that *total* casualties (combatant and noncombatant) were thereby reduced is to miss, or ignore, the point.

9. See Amnesty International, *Report on Torture,* 69.

10. These two categories of torture are not intended to be, and are not, exhaustive.

11. Defenders of privilege customarily portray themselves as defenders of civilization against the vilest barbarians. Self-deception sometimes further smooths the way to treating whoever are the current enemies as beneath contempt and certainly unworthy of equal respect as human beings. Consequently, I am reluctant to concede, even as a limiting case, that there are probably rare individuals so wicked as to lack integrity, or anyway to lack any integrity worthy of respect. But what sort of integrity could one have violated by torturing Hitler?

Any very slight qualification here must not, however, be taken as a flinging wide open of the doors. To be beyond the pale in the relevant respect must involve far more than simply serving values which the torturers find abhorrent. Otherwise, license has been granted simply to torture whoever are one's greatest enemies—the only victims very many torturers would want in any case. Unfortunately, I cannot see a way to delimit those who are genuinely beyond the pale which does not beg for abuse.

12. For a realistic account of the effects of torture, see *Evidence of Torture: Studies by the Amnesty International Danish Medical Group* (London: Amnesty International, 1977). Note in particular: "Undoubtedly the worst sequelae of torture were psychological and neurological" (12). For suggestions about medical ethics for physicians attending persons being tortured, see "Declaration of Tokyo: Guidelines for Medical Doctors Concerning Torture," in United Nations, General Assembly, Note by the Secretary-General, *Torture and other Cruel, Inhuman or Degrading Treatment or Punishment in relation to Detention and Imprisonment* (UN Document A/31/234, 6 October 1976, 31st Session), annex 2.

⚙ REVIEW QUESTIONS

1. What is the argument for permitting torture? According to Shue, what is the weakness of this argument?
2. How does Shue explain the distinction between combatants and noncombatants? What general moral principles are involved?
3. What is in part the basis for the peculiar disgust evoked by torture according to Shue?
4. Explain Shue's distinction between terroristic and interrogational torture.
5. Shue divides possible victims of torture into three categories. What are they, and how are they different?
6. In what case is interrogational torture permissible according to Shue? Explain his reservations about the case.

⚙ DISCUSSION QUESTIONS

1. Is torture morally worse than killing innocent civilians in war? What if innocent children are killed? Is that worse than torturing a terrorist or not?
2. Do you agree that it is permissible to torture a fanatic to save Paris from being destroyed by a nuclear bomb? Why or why not?

Liberalism, Torture and the Ticking Bomb

DAVID LUBAN

For biographical information on David Luban, see his reading in Chapter 9.

Luban attacks what he calls the liberal ideology of torture, which on its surface seems to respect human rights and prohibit torture, but at a deeper level accepts torture in hypothetical ticking-bomb cases and ends up creating a torture culture. In Luban's view, the ticking-bomb story rests on so many assumptions that it amounts to an intellectual fraud. The story unrealistically assumes that the authorities know there is a bomb, that they have captured the man who planted it, that the man will talk when tortured, that lives will be saved, and so on. But this is all uncertain in the real world. We are asked to decide between the certainty of cruel torture and the mere possibility of saving lives, by totaling up costs and benefits.

Source: "Liberalism, Torture and the Ticking Bomb" by David Luban from *Virginia Law Review*, October 2005. Reprinted by permission of *Virginia Law Review* via Copyright Clearance Center.

Trying to make a decision in the ticking-bomb case is just a mistake. The wise course is to deny that it is possible or at least so unlikely that trying to make a decision is insane and frivolous. Furthermore, once we grant the permissibility of torture in a hypothetical case, we end up in the real world with a torture culture that includes trained torturers and prisons like Abu Ghraib.

INTRODUCTION

Torture used to be incompatible with American values. Our Bill of Rights forbids cruel and unusual punishment, and that has come to include all forms of corporal punishment except prison and death by methods purported to be painless. Americans and our government have historically condemned states that torture; we have granted asylum or refuge to those who fear it. The Senate ratified the Convention Against Torture, Congress enacted anti-torture legislation, and judicial opinions spoke of "the dastardly and totally inhuman act of torture."

Then came September 11. Less than one week later, a feature story reported that a quiz in a university ethics class "gave four choices for the proper U.S. response to the terrorist attacks: A.) execute the perpetrators on sight; B.) bring them back for trial in the United States; C.) subject the perpetrators to an international tribunal; or D.) torture and interrogate those involved." Most students chose A and D—execute them on sight and torture them. Six weeks after September 11, the press reported that frustrated FBI interrogators were considering harsh interrogation tactics; a few weeks after that, the *New York Times* reported that torture had become a topic of conversation "in bars, on commuter trains, and at dinner tables." By mid-November 2001, the *Christian Science Monitor* found that thirty-two percent of surveyed Americans favored torturing terror suspects. Alan Dershowitz reported in 2002 that "[d]uring numerous public appearances since September 11, 2001, I have asked audiences for a show of hands as to how many would support the use of nonlethal torture in a ticking-bomb case. Virtually every hand is raised." American abhorrence to torture now appears to have extraordinarily shallow roots.

To an important extent, one's stance on torture runs independent of progressive or conservative ideology. Alan Dershowitz suggests that torture should be regulated by a judicial warrant requirement. Liberal Senator Charles Schumer has publicly rejected the idea "that torture should never, ever be used." He argues that most U.S. senators would back torture to find out where a ticking time bomb is planted. By contrast, William Safire, a self-described "conservative . . . and card-carrying hard-liner," expresses revulsion at "phony-tough" pro-torture arguments, and forthrightly labels torture "barbarism." Examples like these illustrate how vital it is to avoid a simple left-right reductionism. For the most part, American conservatives belong no less than progressives to liberal culture, broadly understood. Henceforth, when I speak of "liberalism," I mean it in the broad sense used by political philosophers from John Stuart Mill on, a sense that includes conservatives as well as progressives, so long as they believe in limited government and the importance of human dignity and individual rights. . . .

On its surface, liberal reverence for individual rights makes torture morally unacceptable; at a deeper level, the same liberal ideas seemingly can justify interrogational torture in the face of danger. These ideas allow us to construct a liberal ideology of torture, by which liberals reassure themselves that essential interrogational torture is detached from its illiberal roots. The liberal ideology of torture is expressed perfectly in so-called "ticking-bomb hypotheticals" designed to show that even perfectly compassionate liberals (like Senator Schumer) might justify torture to find the ticking bomb.

I will criticize the liberal ideology of torture and suggest that ticking-bomb stories are built on a set of assumptions that amount to intellectual fraud. Ticking-bomb stories depict torture as an emergency exception, but use intuitions based on the exceptional case to justify institutionalized practices and procedures of torture. In short, the ticking bomb begins by denying that torture belongs to liberal culture, and ends by constructing a torture culture...

THE TICKING BOMB

Suppose the bomb is planted somewhere in the crowded heart of an American city, and you have custody of the man who planted it. He won't talk. Surely, the hypothetical suggests, we shouldn't be too squeamish to torture the information out of him and save hundreds of lives. Consequences count, and abstract moral prohibitions must yield to the calculus of consequences.

Everyone argues the pros and cons of torture through the ticking time bomb. Senator Schumer and Professor Dershowitz, the Israeli Supreme Court and indeed every journalist devoting a think-piece to the unpleasant question of torture, begins with the ticking time bomb and ends there as well. The Schlesinger Report on Abu Ghraib notes that "[f]or the U.S., most cases for permitting harsh treatment of detainees on moral grounds begin with variants of the 'ticking time-bomb' scenario." At this point in my argument, I mean to disarm the ticking time bomb and argue that it is the wrong thing to think about. If so, then the liberal ideology of torture begins to unravel.

But before beginning these arguments, I want to pause and ask why this jejune example has become the alpha and omega of our thinking about torture. I believe the answer is this: The ticking time bomb is proffered against liberals who believe in an absolute prohibition against torture. The idea is to force the liberal prohibitionist to admit that yes, even he or even she would agree to torture in at least this one situation. Once the prohibitionist admits that, then she has conceded that her opposition to torture is not based on principle. Now that the prohibitionist has admitted that her moral principles can be breached, all that is left is haggling about the price. No longer can the prohibitionist claim the moral high ground; no longer can she

put the burden of proof on her opponent. She is down in the mud with them, and the only question left is how much further down she will go. Dialectically, getting the prohibitionist to address the ticking time bomb is like getting the vegetarian to eat just one little oyster because it has no nervous system. Once she does that— *gotcha!*

The ticking time-bomb scenario serves a second rhetorical goal, one that is equally important to the proponent of torture. It makes us see the torturer in a different light—one of the essential points in the liberal ideology of torture because it is the way that liberals can reconcile themselves to torture even while continuing to "put cruelty first." Now, he is not a cruel man or a sadistic man or a coarse, insensitive brutish man. The torturer is instead a conscientious public servant, heroic the way that New York firefighters were heroic, willing to do desperate things only because the plight is so desperate and so many innocent lives are weighing on the public servant's conscience. The time bomb clinches the great divorce between torture and cruelty; it placates liberals, who put cruelty first.

Wittgenstein once wrote that confusion arises when we become bewitched by a picture. He meant that it's easy to get seduced by simplistic examples that look compelling but actually misrepresent the world in which we live. If the subject is the morality of torture, philosophical confusions can have life-or-death consequences. I believe the ticking time bomb is the picture that bewitches us.

I don't mean that the time-bomb scenario is completely unreal. To take a real-life counterpart: in 1995, an al Qaeda plot to bomb eleven U.S. airliners and assassinate the Pope was thwarted by information tortured out of a Pakistani bomb-maker by the Philippine police. According to journalists Marites Dañguilan Vitug and Glenda M. Gloria, the police had received word of possible threats against the Pope. They went to work. "For weeks, agents hit him with a chair and a long piece of wood, forced water into his mouth, and crushed lighted cigarettes into his private parts.... His ribs were almost totally broken that his captors were surprised that he survived.... Grisly, to be sure—but if they hadn't done it, thousands of innocent travelers might have died horrible deaths.

But look at the example one more time. The Philippine agents were surprised he survived—in other words, they came close to torturing him to death *before* he talked. And they tortured him *for weeks*, during which time they didn't know about any specific al Qaeda plot. What if he too didn't know? Or what if there had been no al Qaeda plot? Then they would have tortured him for weeks, possibly tortured him to death, for nothing. For all they knew at the time, that is exactly what they were doing. You cannot use the argument that preventing the al Qaeda attack justified the decision to torture, because *at the moment the decision was made* no one knew about the al Qaeda attack.

The ticking-bomb scenario cheats its way around these difficulties by stipulating that the bomb is there, ticking away, and that officials know it and know they have the man who planted it. Those conditions will seldom be met. Let us try some more realistic hypotheticals and the questions they raise:

1. The authorities know there may be a bomb plot in the offing, and they have captured a man who may know something about it, but may not. Torture him? How much? For weeks? For months? The chances are considerable that you are torturing a man with nothing to tell you. If he doesn't talk, does that mean it's time to stop, or time to ramp up the level of torture? How likely does it have to be that he knows something important? Fifty-fifty? Thirty-seventy? Will one out of a hundred suffice to land him on the waterboard?

2. Do you really want to make the torture decision by running the numbers? A one-percent chance of saving a thousand lives yields ten statistical lives. Does that mean that you can torture up to nine people on a one-percent chance of finding crucial information?

3. The authorities think that one out of a group of fifty captives in Guantanamo might know where Osama bin Laden is hiding, but they do not know which captive. Torture them

all? That is: Do you torture forty-nine captives with nothing to tell you on the uncertain chance of capturing bin Laden?

4. For that matter, would capturing Osama bin Laden demonstrably save a single human life? The Bush administration has downplayed the importance of capturing bin Laden because American strategy has succeeded in marginalizing him. Maybe capturing him would save lives, but how certain do you have to be? Or does it not matter whether torture is intended to save human lives from a specific threat, as long as it furthers some goal in the War on Terror? This last question is especially important once we realize that the interrogation of al Qaeda suspects will almost never be employed to find out where the ticking bomb is hidden. Instead, interrogation is a more general fishing expedition for any intelligence that might be used to help "unwind" the terrorist organization. Now one might reply that al Qaeda is itself the ticking time bomb, so that unwinding the organization meets the formal conditions of the ticking-bomb hypothetical. This is equivalent to asserting that any intelligence that promotes victory in the War on Terror justifies torture, precisely because we understand that the enemy in the War on Terror aims to kill American civilians. Presumably, on this argument, Japan would have been justified in torturing American captives in World War II on the chance of finding intelligence that would help them shoot down the Enola Gay; I assume that a ticking-bomb hard-liner will not flinch from this conclusion. But at this point, we verge on declaring all military threats and adversaries that menace American civilians to be ticking bombs whose defeat justifies torture. The limitation of torture to emergency exceptions, implicit in the ticking-bomb story, now threatens to unravel, making torture a legitimate instrument of military policy. And then the question becomes inevitable: Why not torture in pursuit of any worthwhile goal?

5. Indeed, if you are willing to torture forty-nine innocent people to get information from the one who has it, why stop there? If suspects will not break under torture, why not torture their loved ones in front of them? They are no more

innocent than the forty-nine you have already shown you are prepared to torture. In fact, if only the numbers matter, torturing loved ones is almost a no-brainer if you think it will work. Of course, you won't know until you try whether torturing his child will break the suspect. But that just changes the odds; it does not alter the argument.

The point of the examples is that in a world of uncertainty and imperfect knowledge, the ticking-bomb scenario should not form the point of reference. The ticking bomb is the picture that bewitches us. The real debate is not between one guilty man's pain and hundreds of innocent lives. It is the debate between the certainty of anguish and the mere possibility of learning something vital and saving lives. And, above all, it is the question about whether a responsible citizen must unblinkingly think the unthinkable and accept that the morality of torture should be decided purely by totaling up costs and benefits. Once you accept that only the numbers count, then anything, no matter how gruesome, becomes possible. "Consequentialist rationality," as Bernard Williams notes sardonically, "will have something to say even on the difference between massacring seven million, and massacring seven million and one."

I am inclined to think that the path of wisdom instead lies in Holocaust survivor David Rousset's famous caution that normal human beings do *not* know that everything is possible. As Williams says, "there are certain situations so monstrous that the idea that the processes of moral rationality could yield an answer in them is insane" and "to spend time thinking what one would decide if one were in such a situation is also insane, if not merely frivolous."

TORTURE AS A PRACTICE

There is a second, insidious, error built into the ticking-bomb hypothetical. It assumes a single, ad hoc decision about whether to torture, by officials who ordinarily would do no such thing except in a desperate emergency. But in the real world of interrogations, decisions are not made

one-off. The real world is a world of policies, guidelines, and directives. It is a world of *practices,* not of ad hoc emergency measures. Therefore, any responsible discussion of torture must address the practice of torture, not the ticking-bomb hypothetical. I am not saying anything original here; other writers have made exactly this point. But somehow, we always manage to forget this and circle back to the ticking time bomb. Its rhetorical power has made it indispensable to the sensitive liberal soul, and we would much rather talk about the ticking bomb than about torture as an organized social practice.

Treating torture as a practice rather than as a desperate improvisation in an emergency means changing the subject from the ticking bomb to other issues like these: Should we create a professional cadre of trained torturers? That means a group of interrogators who know the techniques, who learn to overcome their instinctive revulsion against causing physical pain, and who acquire the legendary surgeon's arrogance about their own infallibility. It has happened before. Medieval executioners were schooled in the arts of agony as part of the trade: how to break men on the wheel, how to rack them, and even how to surreptitiously strangle them as an act of mercy without the bloodthirsty crowd catching on. In Louis XVI's Paris, torture was a hereditary family trade whose tricks were passed on from father to son. Who will teach torture techniques now? Should universities create an undergraduate course in torture? Or should the subject be offered only in police and military academies? Do we want federal grants for research to devise new and better techniques? Patents issued on high-tech torture devices? Companies competing to manufacture them? Trade conventions in Las Vegas? Should there be a medical sub-specialty of torture doctors, who ensure that captives do not die before they talk? The questions amount to this: Do we really want to create a torture culture and the kind of people who inhabit it? The ticking time bomb distracts us from the real issue, which is not about emergencies, but about the normalization of torture.

Perhaps the solution is to keep the practice of torture secret in order to avoid the moral corruption that comes from creating a public culture of torture. But this so-called "solution" does not reject the normalization of torture. It accepts it, but layers on top of it the normalization of state secrecy. The result would be a shadow culture of torturers and those who train and support them, operating outside the public eye and accountable only to other insiders of the torture culture.

Just as importantly: Who guarantees that case-hardened torturers, inured to levels of violence and pain that would make ordinary people vomit at the sight, will know where to draw the line on when torture should be used? They rarely have in the past. They didn't in Algeria. They didn't in Israel, where in 1999, the Israeli Supreme Court backpedaled from an earlier consent to torture lite because the interrogators were running amok and torturing two-thirds of their Palestinian captives. In the Argentinian Dirty War, the tortures began because terrorist cells had a policy of fleeing when one of their members had disappeared for forty-eight hours, leaving authorities two days to wring the information out of the captive. Mark Osiel, who has studied the Argentinean military in the Dirty War, reports that many of the torturers initially had qualms about what they were doing, until their priests reassured them that they were fighting God's fight. By the end of the Dirty War, the qualms were gone, and, as John Simpson and Jana Bennett report, hardened young officers were placing bets on who could kidnap the prettiest girl to rape and torture. Escalation is the rule, not the aberration.

There are two fundamental reasons for this: one rooted in the nature of bureaucracy and the other in social psychology. The liberal ideology of torture presupposes a torturer impelled by the desire to stop a looming catastrophe, not by cruelty. Implicitly, this image presumes that the interrogator and the decisionmaker are the same person. But the defining fact about real organizations is the division of labor. The person who decides whether this prisoner presents a genuine ticking-bomb case is not the interrogator. The decision about what counts as a ticking-bomb case—one where torture is the lesser evil—depends on complex value judgments, and these are made further up the chain of command. The interrogator simply executes decisions made elsewhere.

Interrogators do not inhabit a world of loving kindness, or of equal concern and respect for all human beings. Interrogating resistant prisoners non-violently and non-abusively still requires a relationship that in any other context would be morally abhorrent. It requires tricking information out of the subject, and the interrogator does this by setting up elaborate scenarios to disorient the subject and propel him into an alternative reality. The subject must be deceived into thinking that his high-value intelligence has already been revealed by someone else, so that it is no longer of any value. He must be fooled into thinking that his friends have betrayed him or that the interrogator is his friend. The interrogator disrupts his sense of time and place, disorients him with sessions that never take place at predictable times or intervals, and manipulates his emotions. The very names of interrogation techniques show this: "Emotional Love," "Emotional Hate," "Fear Up Harsh," "Fear Up Mild," "Reduced Fear," "Pride and Ego Up," "Pride and Ego Down," "Futility." The interrogator may set up a scenario to make the subject think he is in the clutches of a much-feared secret police organization from a different country ("False Flag"). Every bit of the subject's environment is fair game for manipulation and deception, as the interrogator aims to create the total lie that gets the subject talking.

Let me be clear that I am not objecting to these deceptions. None of these practices rises to the level of abuse or torture lite, let alone torture heavy, and surely tricking the subject into talking is legitimate if the goals of the interrogation are legitimate. But what I have described is a relationship of totalitarian mind-control more profound than the world of Orwell's *1984*. The interrogator is like Descartes' Evil Deceiver, and the subject lives in a false reality reminiscent of *The Matrix*. The liberal fiction that interrogation can be done by people who are neither cruel nor tyrannical runs aground on the fact that regardless of the interrogator's character off the job, on the job, every fiber of his concentration is devoted to dominating the mind of the subject.

Only one thing prevents this from turning into abuse and torture, and that is a clear set of bright-line rules, drummed into the interrogator with the intensity of a religious indoctrination, complete with warnings of fire and brimstone. American interrogator Chris Mackey reports that warnings about the dire consequences of violating the Geneva Conventions "were repeated so often that by the end of our time at [training school] the three syllables 'Leaven-worth' were ringing in our ears."

But what happens when the line is breached? When, as in Afghanistan, the interrogator gets mixed messages about whether Geneva applies, or hears rumors of ghost detainees, of high-value captives held for years of interrogation in the top-secret facility known as "Hotel California," located in some nation somewhere? Or when the interrogator observes around him the move from deception to abuse, from abuse to torture lite, from torture lite to beatings and waterboarding? Without clear lines, the tyranny innate in the interrogator's job has nothing to hold it in check. Perhaps someone, somewhere in the chain of command, is wringing hands over whether this interrogation qualifies as a ticking-bomb case; but the interrogator knows only that the rules of the road have changed and the posted speed limits no longer apply. The liberal fiction of the conscientious interrogator overlooks a division of moral labor in which the person with the fastidious conscience and the person doing the interrogation are not the same.

The fiction must presume, therefore, that the interrogator operates only under the strictest supervision, in a chain of command where his every move gets vetted and controlled by the superiors who are actually doing the deliberating. The trouble is that this assumption flies in the face of everything that we know about how organizations work. The basic rule in every bureaucratic organization is that operational details and the guilty knowledge that goes with them get pushed down the chain of command as far as possible. As sociologist Robert Jackall explains,

[i]t is characteristic ... that details are pushed down and credit is pulled up. Superiors do not like to give detailed instructions to subordinates. . . . [O]ne of the privileges of authority is the divestment of humdrum intricacies. . . . Perhaps more important, pushing details down protects the privilege of authority to declare that a mistake has been made. . . . Moreover, pushing down details relieves superiors of the burden of too much knowledge, particularly guilty knowledge.

We saw this phenomenon at Abu Ghraib, where military intelligence officers gave military police vague orders like: " 'Loosen this guy up for us;' 'Make sure he has a bad night.' 'Make sure he gets the treatment.' "Suppose that the eighteen-year-old guard interprets "[m]ake sure he has a bad night" to mean, simply, "keep him awake all night." How do you do that without physical abuse? Furthermore, personnel at Abu Ghraib witnessed far harsher treatment of prisoners by "other governmental agencies" (OGA), a euphemism for the Central Intelligence Agency. They saw OGA spirit away the dead body of an interrogation subject, and allegedly witnessed a contract employee rape a youthful prisoner. When that is what you see, abuses like those in the Abu Ghraib photos will not look outrageous. Outrageous compared with what?

This brings me to the point of social psychology. Simply stated, it is this: we judge right and wrong against the baseline of whatever we have come to consider "normal" behavior, and if the norm shifts in the direction of violence, we will come to tolerate and accept violence as a normal response. The psychological mechanisms for this re-normalization have been studied for more than half a century, and by now they are reasonably well understood. Rather than detour into psychological theory, however, I will illustrate the point with the most salient example—one that seems so obviously applicable to Abu Ghraib that the Schlesinger Commission discussed it at length in an appendix to its report. This is the famous Stanford Prison Experiment. Male volunteers were divided randomly into two groups who would simulate the guards and inmates in a mock prison. Within a matter of days, the inmates began acting like actual prison inmates—depressed, enraged, and anxious. And the guards began to abuse the inmates to such an alarming degree that the researchers had to halt the two-week experiment after just seven days. In the words of the experimenters:

> The use of power was self-aggrandising and self-perpetuating. The guard power, derived initially from an arbitrary label, was intensified whenever there was any perceived threat by the prisoners and this new level subsequently became the baseline from which further hostility and harassment would begin. . . . [T]he absolute level of aggression as well as the more subtle and "creative" forms of aggression manifested, increased in a spiralling function.

It took only five days before a guard, who prior to the experiment described himself as a pacifist, was forcing greasy sausages down the throat of a prisoner who refused to eat; and in less than a week, the guards were placing bags over prisoners' heads, making them strip, and sexually humiliating them in ways reminiscent of Abu Ghraib.

My conclusion is very simple. Abu Ghraib is the fully predictable image of what a torture culture looks like. Abu Ghraib is not a few bad apples—it is the apple tree. And you cannot reasonably expect that interrogators in a torture culture will be the fastidious and well-meaning torturers that the liberal ideology fantasizes.

This is why Alan Dershowitz has argued that judges, not torturers, should oversee the permission to torture, which in his view must be regulated by warrants. The irony is that Jay S. Bybee, who signed the Justice Department's highly permissive torture memo, is now a federal judge. Politicians pick judges, and if the politicians accept torture, the judges will as well. Once we create a torture culture, only the naive would suppose that judges will provide a safeguard. Judges do not fight their culture—they reflect it.

For all these reasons, the ticking-bomb scenario is an intellectual fraud. In its place, we must address the real questions about torture—questions about uncertainty, questions about the morality of consequences, and questions about what it does to a culture and the torturers themselves to introduce the practice. Once we do so, I suspect that few Americans will be willing to accept that everything is possible.

REVIEW QUESTIONS

1. What happened to the American view of torture after 9/11 according to Luban?
2. How does Luban define "liberalism"? Who is a liberal on his definition?
3. Explain Luban's view of the "liberal ideology of torture."
4. What is the basic ticking-bomb story? According to Luban, what assumptions does the story make? What questions are left unanswered?
5. Besides being unrealistic, what second error is built into the ticking-bomb story?
6. What is Luban's point about the Stanford Prison Experiment?

DISCUSSION QUESTIONS

1. Does the ticking-bomb story amount to intellectual fraud, as Luban says? Or does it describe a situation that could actually happen? What is your view?
2. Should we train professional torturers so that we will be able to effectively torture terrorists to get information about possible or actual attacks?

How to Interrogate Terrorists

HEATHER MACDONALD

Heather MacDonald is a John M. Olin fellow at the Manhattan Institute and a contributing editor to *City Journal*. She is the author of *Are Cops Racist?* (2003), *The Burden of Bad Ideas* (2000), and many writings in newspapers on a variety of topics, including homeland security, immigration, and homelessness.

MacDonald argues that to succeed in the war on terrorism, the military must be allowed to use stress techniques on unlawful combatants such as sleep deprivation, loud noise, prolonged kneeling or standing, grabbing, poking in the chest with a finger, light pushing, and so on. According to MacDonald, none of these techniques comes close to torture or cruel or degrading treatment. As for Abu Ghraib, what went on there was the result the chaos of the war and has nothing to do with approved interrogation techniques.

It didn't take long for interrogators in the war on terror to realize that their part was not going according to script. Pentagon doctrine, honed over decades of cold-war planning, held that 95 percent of prisoners would break upon straightforward questioning. Interrogators in Afghanistan, and later in Cuba and Iraq, found just the opposite: virtually none of the terror detainees was giving up information—not in response to direct questioning, and not in response to army-approved psychological gambits for prisoners of war.

Debate erupted in detention centers across the globe about how to get detainees to talk. Were "stress techniques"—such as isolation or sleep deprivation to decrease a detainee's resistance to questioning—acceptable? Before the discussion concluded, however, the photos of prisoner abuse in Iraq's Abu Ghraib prison appeared. Though they showed the sadism of a prison out of control, they showed nothing about interrogation.

Nevertheless, Bush-administration critics seized on the scandal as proof that prisoner "torture" had become routine. A master narrative—call it the "torture narrative"—sprang up: the government's 2002 decision to deny Geneva-convention status to al-Qaida fighters, it held,

"led directly to the abuse of detainees in Afghanistan and Iraq," to quote the *Washington Post*. In particular, torturous interrogation methods, developed at Guantánamo Bay and Afghanistan in illegal disregard of Geneva protections, migrated to Abu Ghraib and were manifest in the abuse photos.

This story's success depends on the reader's remaining ignorant of the actual interrogation techniques promulgated in the war on terror. Not only were they light years from real torture and hedged around with bureaucratic safeguards, but they had nothing to do with the Abu Ghraib anarchy. Moreover, the decision on the Geneva conventions was irrelevant to interrogation practices in Iraq.

No matter. The Pentagon's reaction to the scandal was swift and sweeping. It stripped interrogators not just of stress options but of traditional techniques long regarded as uncontroversial as well. Red tape now entangles the interrogation process, and detainees know that their adversaries' hands are tied.

The need for rethinking interrogation doctrine in the war on terror will not go away, however. The Islamist enemy is unlike any the military has encountered in the past. If current wisdom on

Source: "How to Interrogate Terrorists" by Heather MacDonald from *City Journal*, Winter 2005, pp. 1–8. Reprinted by permission of *City Journal*.

the rules of war prohibits making any distinction between a terrorist and a lawful combatant, then that orthodoxy needs to change.

The interrogation debate first broke out on the frigid plains of Afghanistan. Marines and other special forces would dump planeloads of al-Qaida and Taliban prisoners into a ramshackle detention facility outside the Kandahar airport; waiting interrogators were then supposed to extract information to be fed immediately back into the battlefield—whether a particular mountain pass was booby-trapped, say, or where an arms cache lay. That "tactical" debriefing accomplished, the Kandahar interrogation crew would determine which prisoners were significant enough to be shipped on to the Guantánamo naval base in Cuba for high-level interrogation.

Army doctrine gives interrogators 16 "approaches" to induce prisoners of war to divulge critical information. Sporting names like "Pride and Ego Down" and "Fear Up Harsh," these approaches aim to exploit a detainee's self-love, allegiance to or resentment of comrades, or sense of futility. Applied in the right combination, they will work on nearly everyone, the intelligence soldiers had learned in their training.

But the Kandahar prisoners were not playing by the army rule book. They divulged nothing. "Prisoners overcame the [traditional] model almost effortlessly," writes Chris Mackey in *The Interrogators,* his gripping account of his interrogation service in Afghanistan. The prisoners confounded their captors "not with clever cover stories but with simple refusal to cooperate. They offered lame stories, pretended not to remember even the most basic of details, and then waited for consequences that never really came."

Some of the al-Qaida fighters had received resistance training, which taught that Americans were strictly limited in how they could question prisoners. Failure to cooperate, the al-Qaida manuals revealed, carried no penalties and certainly no risk of torture—a sign, gloated the manuals, of American weakness.

Even if a prisoner had not previously studied American detention policies before arriving at Kandahar, he soon figured them out. "It became very clear very early on to the detainees that the Americans were just going to have them sit there," recalls interrogator Joe Martin (a pseudonym). "They realized: 'The Americans will give us our Holy Book, they'll draw lines on the floor showing us where to pray, we'll get three meals a day with fresh fruit, do Jazzercise with the guards,... we can wait them out.' "

Even more challenging was that these detainees bore little resemblance to traditional prisoners of war. The army's interrogation manual presumed adversaries who were essentially the mirror image of their captors, motivated by emotions that all soldiers share. A senior intelligence official who debriefed prisoners in the 1989 U.S. operation in Panama contrasts the battlefield then and now: "There were no martyrs down there, believe me," he chuckles. "The Panamanian forces were more understandable people for us. Interrogation was pretty straightforward: 'Love of Family' [an army-manual approach, promising, say, contact with wife or children in exchange for cooperation] or, 'Here's how you get out of here as fast as you can.' "

"Love of family" often had little purchase among the terrorists, however—as did love of life. "The jihadists would tell you, 'I've divorced this life, I don't care about my family,' " recalls an interrogator at Guantánamo. "You couldn't shame them." The fierce hatred that the captives bore their captors heightened their resistance. The U.S. ambassador to Pakistan reported in January 2002 that prisoners in Kandahar would "shout epithets at their captors, including threats against the female relatives of the soldiers guarding them, knee marines in the groin, and say that they will escape and kill 'more Americans and Jews.' " Such animosity continued in Guantánamo.

Battlefield commanders in Afghanistan and intelligence officials in Washington kept pressing for information, however. The frustrated interrogators constantly discussed how to get it. The best hope, they agreed, was to re-create the "shock of capture"—that vulnerable mental state when a prisoner is most frightened, most uncertain, and most likely to respond to questioning. Uncertainty is an interrogator's most powerful ally; exploited wisely, it can lead the detainee to believe that the interrogator is in total control and holds the key to his future. The Kandahar detainees, however, learned almost immediately what their future held, no matter how egregious their behavior: nothing untoward.

Many of the interrogators argued for a calibrated use of "stress techniques"—long interrogations that would cut into the detainees' sleep schedules, for example, or making a prisoner kneel or stand, or aggressive questioning that would put a detainee on edge.

Joe Martin—a crack interrogator who discovered that a top al-Qaida leader, whom Pakistan claimed to have in custody, was still at large and directing the Afghani resistance—explains the psychological effect of stress: "Let's say a detainee comes into the interrogation booth and he's had resistance training. He knows that I'm completely handcuffed and that I can't do anything to him. If I throw a temper tantrum, lift him onto his knees, and walk out, you can feel his uncertainty level rise dramatically. He's been told: 'They won't physically touch you,' and now you have. The point is not to beat him up but to introduce the reality into his mind that he doesn't know where your limit is." Grabbing someone by the top of the collar has had a more profound effect on the outcome of questioning than any actual torture could have, Martin maintains. "The guy knows: You just broke your own rules, and that's scary. He might demand to talk to my supervisor. I'll respond: 'There are no supervisors here,' and give him a maniacal smile."

The question was: Was such treatment consistent with the Geneva conventions?

President Bush had declared in February 2002 that al-Qaida members fell wholly outside the conventions and that Taliban prisoners would not receive prisoner-of-war status—without which they, too, would not be covered by the Geneva rules. Bush ordered, however, that detainees be treated humanely and in accordance with Geneva principles, to the extent consistent with military necessity. This second

pronouncement sank in: all of the war on terror's detention facilities chose to operate under Geneva rules. Contrary to the fulminations of rights advocates and the press, writes Chris Mackey, "Every signal we interrogators got from above from the colonels at [the Combined Forces Land Component Command] in Kuwait to the officers at Central Command back in Tampa—had been...to observe the Conventions, respect prisoners' rights, and never cut corners."

What emerged was a hybrid and fluid set of detention practices. As interrogators tried to overcome the prisoners' resistance, their reference point remained Geneva and other humanitarian treaties. But the interrogators pushed into the outer limits of what they thought the law allowed, undoubtedly recognizing that the prisoners in their control violated everything the pacts stood for.

The Geneva conventions embody the idea that even in as brutal an activity as war, civilized nations could obey humanitarian rules: no attacking civilians and no retaliation against enemy soldiers once they fall into your hands. Destruction would be limited as much as possible to professional soldiers on the battlefield. That rule required, unconditionally, that soldiers distinguish themselves from civilians by wearing uniforms and carrying arms openly.

Obedience to Geneva rules rests on another bedrock moral principle: reciprocity. Nations will treat an enemy's soldiers humanely because they want and expect their adversaries to do the same. Terrorists flout every civilized norm animating the conventions. Their whole purpose is to kill noncombatants, to blend into civilian populations, and to conceal their weapons. They pay no heed whatever to the golden rule; anyone who falls into their hands will most certainly not enjoy commissary privileges and wages, per the Geneva mandates. He—or she—may even lose his head.

Even so, terror interrogators tried to follow the spirit of the Geneva code for conventional, uniformed prisoners of war. That meant, as the code puts it, that the detainees could not be tortured or subjected to "any form of coercion" in order to secure information. They were to be "humanely" treated, protected against "unpleasant or disadvantageous treatment of any kind," and were entitled to "respect for their persons and their honour."

The Kandahar interrogators reached the following rule of thumb, reports Mackey: if a type of behavior toward a prisoner was no worse than the way the army treated its own members, it could not be considered torture or a violation of the conventions. Thus, questioning a detainee past his bedtime was lawful as long as his interrogator stayed up with him. If the interrogator was missing exactly the same amount of sleep as the detainee—and no tag-teaming of interrogators would be allowed, the soldiers decided—then sleep deprivation could not be deemed torture. In fact, interrogators were routinely sleep-deprived, catnapping maybe one or two hours a night, even as the detainees were getting long beauty sleeps. Likewise, if a boot-camp drill sergeant can make a recruit kneel with his arms stretched out in front without violating the Convention Against Torture, an interrogator can use that tool against a recalcitrant terror suspect.

Did the stress techniques work? Yes. "The harsher methods we used ... the better information we got and the sooner we got it," writes Mackey, who emphasizes that the methods never contravened the conventions or crossed over into torture. . . .

But there is a huge gray area between the gold standard of POW treatment reserved for honorable opponents and torture, which consists of the intentional infliction of severe physical and mental pain. None of the stress techniques that the military has used in the war on terror comes remotely close to torture, despite the hysterical charges of administration critics. (The CIA's behavior remains a black box.) To declare non-torturous stress off-limits for an enemy who plays by no rules and accords no respect to Western prisoners is folly.

The soldiers used stress techniques to reinforce the traditional psychological approaches. Jeff (a pseudonym), an interrogator in Afghanistan, had been assigned a cocky English Muslim, who justified the 9/11 attacks because women had been working in the World Trade Center. The

British citizen deflected all further questioning. Jeff questioned him for a day and a half, without letting him sleep and playing on his religious loyalties. "I broke him on his belief in Islam," Jeff recounts. "He realized he had messed up, because his Muslim brothers and sisters were also in the building." The Brit broke down and cried, then disclosed the mission that al-Qaida had put him on before capture. But once the prisoner was allowed to sleep for six hours, he again "clammed up."

Halfway across the globe, an identical debate had broken out, among interrogators who were encountering the same obstacles as the Afghanistan intelligence team. The U.S. base at Guantánamo was supposed to be getting the Afghanistan war's worst of the worst: the al-Qaida Arabs and their high Taliban allies.

Usama bin Ladin's driver and bodyguard were there, along with explosives experts, al-Qaida financiers and recruiters, would-be suicide recruits, and the architects of numerous attacks on civilian targets. They knew about al-Qaida's leadership structure, its communication methods, and its plans to attack the U.S. And they weren't talking. "They'd laugh at you; 'You've asked me this before,' they'd say contemptuously," reports Major General Michael Dunlavey, a former Guantánamo commanding officer. "Their resistance was tenacious. They'd already had 90 days in Afghanistan to get their cover stories together and to plan with their compatriots."

Even more than Afghanistan, Guantánamo dissipated any uncertainty the detainees might have had about the consequences of noncooperation. Consistent with the president's call for humane treatment, prisoners received expert medical care, three culturally appropriate meals each day, and daily opportunities for prayer, showers, and exercise. They had mail privileges and reading materials. Their biggest annoyance was boredom, recalls one interrogator. Many prisoners disliked the move from Camp X-Ray, the first facility used at the base, to the more commodious Camp Delta, because it curtailed their opportunities for homosexual sex, says an intelligence analyst. The captives protested every perceived infringement of their rights but, as in

Afghanistan, ignored any reciprocal obligation. They hurled excrement and urine at guards, used their blankets as garrotes, and created additional weapons out of anything they could get their hands on—including a sink wrenched off a wall. Guards who responded to the attacks—with pepper spray or a water hose, say—got punished and, in one case, court-martialed.

Gitmo personnel disagreed sharply over what tools interrogators could legally use. The FBI took the most conservative position. When a bureau agent questioning Mohamedou Ould Slahi—a Mauritanian al-Qaida operative who had recruited two of the 9/11 pilots—was getting nothing of value, an army interrogator suggested, "Why don't you mention to him that conspiracy is a capital offense?" "That would be a violation of the Convention Against Torture," shot back the agent—on the theory that any covert threat inflicts "severe mental pain." Never mind that district attorneys and police detectives routinely invoke the possibility of harsh criminal penalties to get criminals to confess. Federal prosecutors in New York have even been known to remind suspects that they are more likely to keep their teeth and not end up as sex slaves by pleading to a federal offense, thus avoiding New York City's Rikers Island jail. Using such a method against an al-Qaida jihadist, by contrast, would be branded a serious humanitarian breach.

Top military commanders often matched the FBI's restraint, however. "It was ridiculous the things we couldn't do," recalls an army interrogator. "One guy said he would talk if he could see the ocean. It wasn't approved, because it would be a change of scenery"—a privilege that discriminated in favor of a cooperating detainee, as opposed to being available to all, regardless of their behavior.

Frustration with prisoner stonewalling reached a head with Mohamed al-Kahtani, a Saudi who had been fighting with Usama bin Ladin's bodyguards in Afghanistan in December 2001. By July 2002, analysts had figured out that Kahtani was the missing 20th hijacker. He had flown into Orlando International Airport from Dubai on August 4, 2001, but a sharp-eyed customs agent had denied him entry. Waiting for him at the other side of the gate was Mohamed Atta.

Kahtani's resistance strategies were flawless. Around the first anniversary of 9/11, urgency to get information on al-Qaida grew. Finally, army officials at Guantánamo prepared a legal analysis of their interrogation options and requested permission from Defense Secretary Donald Rumsfeld to use various stress techniques on Kahtani. Their memo, sent up the bureaucratic chain on October 11, 2002, triggered a fierce six-month struggle in Washington among military lawyers, administration officials, and Pentagon chiefs about interrogation in the war on terror.

To read the techniques requested is to understand how restrained the military has been in its approach to terror detainees—and how utterly false the torture narrative has been. Here's what the interrogators assumed they could not do without clearance from the secretary of defense: yell at detainees (though never in their ears), use deception (such as posing as Saudi intelligence agents), and put detainees on MREs (meals ready to eat—vacuum-sealed food pouches eaten by millions of soldiers, as well as vacationing backpackers) instead of hot rations. The interrogators promised that this dangerous dietary measure would be used only *in extremis,* pending local approval and special training.

The most controversial technique approved was "mild, non-injurious physical contact such as grabbing, poking in the chest with the finger, and light pushing," to be reserved only for a "very small percentage of the most uncooperative detainees" believed to possess critical intelligence. A detainee could be poked only after review by Gitmo's commanding general of intelligence and the commander of the U.S. Southern Command in Miami, and only pursuant to "careful coordination" and monitoring.

None of this remotely approaches torture or cruel or degrading treatment. Nevertheless, fanatically cautious Pentagon lawyers revolted, claiming that the methods approved for Kahtani violated international law. Uncharacteristically irresolute, Rumsfeld rescinded the Guantánamo techniques in January 2003.

Kahtani's interrogation hung fire for three months, while a Washington committee, with representatives from the undersecretary of defense, the Defense Intelligence Agency, the air force, army, navy, and marine corps, and attorneys from every branch of the military, considered how to approach the 20th hijacker.

The outcome of this massive deliberation was more restrictive than the Geneva conventions themselves, even though they were to apply only to unlawful combatants, not conventional prisoners of war, and only to those held at Guantánamo Bay. It is worth scrutinizing the final 24 techniques Rumsfeld approved for terrorists at Gitmo in April 2003, since these are the techniques that the media presents as the source of "torture" at Abu Ghraib. The torture narrative holds that illegal methods used at Guantánamo migrated to Iraq and resulted in the abuse of prisoners there.

So what were these cruel and degrading practices? For one, providing a detainee an incentive for cooperation—such as a cigarette or, especially favored in Cuba, a McDonald's Filet-O-Fish sandwich or a Twinkie unless specifically approved by the secretary of defense. In other words, if an interrogator had learned that Usama bin Ladin's accountant loved Cadbury chocolate, and intended to enter the interrogation booth armed with a Dairy Milk Wafer to extract the name of a Saudi financier, he needed to "specifically determine that military necessity requires" the use of the Dairy Milk Wafer and send an alert to Secretary Rumsfeld that chocolate was to be deployed against an al-Qaida operative.

Similar restrictions—a specific finding of military necessity and notice to Rumsfeld—applied to other tried-and-true army psychological techniques. These included "Pride and Ego Down"—attacking a detainee's pride to goad him into revealing critical information—as well as "Mutt and Jeff," the classic good cop–bad cop routine of countless police shows. Isolating a detainee from other prisoners to prevent collaboration and to increase his need to talk required not just notice and a finding of military

necessity but "detailed implementation instructions [and] medical and psychological review."

The only non-conventional "stress" techniques on the final Guantánamo list are such innocuous interventions as adjusting the temperature or introducing an unpleasant smell into the interrogation room, but only if the interrogator is present at all times; reversing a detainee's sleep cycles from night to day (call this the "Flying to Hong Kong" approach); and convincing a detainee that his interrogator is not from the U.S.

Note that none of the treatments shown in the Abu Ghraib photos, such as nudity or the use of dogs, was included in the techniques certified for the unlawful combatants held in Cuba. And those mild techniques that were certified could only be used with extensive bureaucratic oversight and medical monitoring to ensure "humane," "safe," and "lawful" application.

After Rumsfeld cleared the 24 methods, interrogators approached Kahtani once again. They relied almost exclusively on isolation and lengthy interrogations. They also used some "psy-ops" (psychological operations). Ten or so interrogators would gather and sing the Rolling Stones' "Time Is on My Side" outside Kahtani's cell. Sometimes they would play a recording of "Enter Sandman" by the heavy-metal group Metallica, which brought Kahtani to tears, because he thought (not implausibly) he was hearing the sound of Satan.

Finally, at 4 am—after an 18-hour, occasionally loud, interrogation, during which Kahtani head-butted his interrogators—he started giving up information, convinced that he was being sold out by his buddies. The entire process had been conducted under the watchful eyes of a medic, a psychiatrist, and lawyers, to make sure that no harm was done. Kahtani provided detailed information on his meetings with Usama bin Ladin, on Jose Padilla and Richard Reid, and on Adnan El Shukrijumah, one of the FBI's most wanted terrorists, believed to be wandering between South and North America.

Since then, according to Pentagon officials, none of the non-traditional techniques approved for Kahtani has been used on anyone else at Guantánamo Bay.

The final strand in the "torture narrative" is the least grounded in actual practice, but it has had the most distorting effect on the public debate. In the summer of 2002, the CIA sought legal advice about permissible interrogation techniques for the recently apprehended Abu Zubaydah, Usama bin Ladin's chief recruiter in the 1990s. The Palestinian Zubaydah had already been sentenced to death in absentia in Jordan for an abortive plot to bomb hotels there during the millennium celebration; he had arranged to obliterate the Los Angeles airport on the same night. The CIA wanted to use techniques on Zubaydah that the military uses on marines and other elite fighters in Survive, Evade, Resist, Escape (SERE) school, which teaches how to withstand torture and other pressures to collaborate. The techniques are classified, but none allegedly involves physical contact. (Later, the CIA is said to have used "waterboarding"—temporarily submerging a detainee in water to induce the sensation of drowning—on Khalid Sheik Mohammad, the mastermind of the 9/11 attacks. Water-boarding is the most extreme method the CIA has applied, according to a former Justice Department attorney, and arguably it crosses the line into torture.)

In response to the CIA's request, Assistant Attorney General Jay S. Bybee produced a hairraising memo that understandably caused widespread alarm. Bybee argued that a U.S. law ratifying the 1984 Convention Against Torture—covering all persons, whether lawful combatants or not—forbade only physical pain equivalent to that "accompanying serious physical injury, such as organ failure, impairment of bodily function, or even death," or mental pain that resulted in "significant psychological harm of significant duration, e.g., lasting for months or even years." More troubling still, Bybee concluded that the torture statute and international humanitarian treaties did not bind the executive branch in wartime.

This infamous August "torture memo" represents the high (or low) point of the Bush administration's theory of untrammeled presidential war-making power. But note: it had nothing to do with the interrogation debates and experiments unfolding among Pentagon interrogators in Afghanistan and Cuba. These soldiers struggling with al-Qaida resistance were perfectly ignorant about executive-branch deliberations on the outer boundaries of pain and executive power (which, in any case, were prepared for and seen only by the CIA). "We had no idea what went on in Washington," said Chris Mackey in an interview. A Guantánamo lawyer involved in the Kahtani interrogation echoes Mackey: "We were not aware of the [Justice Department and White House] debates." Interrogators in Iraq were equally unaware of the Bybee memo.

Nevertheless, when the Bybee analysis was released in June 2004, it became the capstone on the torture narrative, the most damning link between the president's decision that the Geneva conventions didn't apply to terrorists and the sadistic behavior of the military guards at Abu Ghraib. Seymour Hersh, the left-wing journalist who broke the Abu Ghraib story, claims that the Bybee torture memo was the "most suggestive document, in terms of what was really going on inside military prisons and detention centers."

But not only is the Bybee memo irrelevant to what happened in Abu Ghraib; so, too, are the previous interrogation debates in Afghanistan and Cuba. The abuse at Abu Ghraib resulted from the Pentagon's failure to plan for any outcome of the Iraq invasion except the most rosy scenario, its failure to respond to the insurgency once it broke out, and its failure to keep military discipline from collapsing in the understaffed Abu Ghraib facility. Interrogation rules were beside the point.

As the avalanche of prisoners taken in the street fighting overwhelmed the inadequate contingent of guards and officers at Abu Ghraib, order within the ranks broke down as thoroughly as order in the operation of the prison itself. Soldiers talked back to their superiors, refused to wear uniforms, operated prostitution and bootlegging rings, engaged in rampant and public sexual misbehavior, covered the facilities with graffiti, and indulged in drinking binges while on duty. No one knew who was in command. The guards' sadistic and sexualized treatment of prisoners was just an extension of the chaos they were already wallowing in with no restraint from above. Meanwhile, prisoners regularly rioted; insurgents shelled the compound almost daily; the army sent only rotten, bug-infested rations; and the Iraqi guards sold favors to the highest bidders among the insurgents.

The idea that the abuse of the Iraqi detainees resulted from the president's decision on the applicability of the Geneva conventions to al-Qaida and Taliban detainees is absurd on several grounds. Everyone in the military chain of command emphasized repeatedly that the Iraq conflict would be governed by the conventions in their entirety. The interrogation rules that local officers developed for Iraq explicitly stated that they were promulgated under Geneva authority, and that the conventions applied. Moreover, almost all the behavior shown in the photographs occurred in the dead of night among military police, wholly separate from interrogations. Most abuse victims were not even scheduled to be interrogated, because they were of no intelligence value. Finally, except for the presence of dogs, none of the behavior shown in the photos was included in the interrogation rules promulgated in Iraq. Mandated masturbation, dog leashes, assault, and stacking naked prisoners in pyramids—none of these depredations was an approved (or even contemplated) interrogation practice, and no interrogator ordered the military guards to engage in them.

It is the case that intelligence officers in Iraq and Afghanistan were making use of nudity and phobias about dogs at the time. Nudity was not officially sanctioned, and the official rule about dogs only allowed their "presence" in the interrogation booth, not their being sicced on naked detainees. The argument that such techniques contributed to a dehumanization of the detainees, which in turn led to their abuse, is not wholly implausible. Whether or not those two particular stressors are worth defending (and many interrogators say they are not), their abuse should not discredit the validity of other stress techniques that the military was cautiously experimenting with in the months before Abu Ghraib.

That experiment is over. Reeling under the PR disaster of Abu Ghraib, the Pentagon shut down every stress technique but one—isolation—and that can be used only after extensive review. An interrogator who so much as requests permission to question a detainee into the night could be putting his career in jeopardy. Even the traditional army psychological approaches have fallen under a deep cloud of suspicion: deflating a detainee's ego, aggressive but nonphysical histrionics, and good cop–bad cop have been banished along with sleep deprivation.

Timidity among officers prevents the energetic application of those techniques that remain. Interrogation plans have to be triple-checked all the way up through the Pentagon by officers who have never conducted an interrogation in their lives.

In losing these techniques, interrogators have lost the ability to create the uncertainty vital to getting terrorist information. Since the Abu Ghraib scandal broke, the military has made public nearly every record of its internal interrogation debates, providing al-Qaida analysts with an encyclopedia of U.S. methods and constraints. Those constraints make perfectly clear that the interrogator is not in control. "In reassuring the world about our limits, we have destroyed our biggest asset: detainee doubt," a senior Pentagon intelligence official laments.

Soldiers on the ground are noticing the consequences. "The Iraqis already know the game. They know how to play us," a marine chief warrant officer told the *Wall Street Journal* in August. "Unless you catch the Iraqis in the act, it is very hard to pin anything on anyone.... We can't even use basic police interrogation tactics."

And now the rights advocates, energized by the Abu Ghraib debacle, are making one final push to halt interrogation altogether. In the *New York Times's* words, the International Committee of the Red Cross (ICRC) is now condemning the thoroughly emasculated interrogation process at Guantánamo Bay as a "system devised to break the will of the prisoners [and] make them wholly dependent on their interrogators." In other words, the ICRC opposes traditional interrogation itself, since *all* interrogation is designed to "break the will of prisoners" and make them feel "dependent on their interrogators." But according to an ICRC report leaked to the *Times*, "the construction of such a system, whose stated purpose is the production of intelligence, cannot be considered other than an intentional system of cruel, unusual and degrading treatment and a form of torture."

But contrary to the fantasies of the international-law and human rights lobbies, a world in which all interrogation is illegal and rights are indiscriminately doled out is not a safer or more just world. Were the United States to announce that terrorists would be protected under the Geneva conventions, it would destroy any incentive our ruthless enemies have to comply with the laws of war. The *Washington Post* and the *New York Times* understood that truth in 1987, when they supported President Ronald Reagan's rejection of an amendment to the Geneva conventions that would have granted lawful-combatant status to terrorists. Today, however, those same opinion makers have done an about-face, though the most striking feature of their denunciations of the Bush administration's Geneva decisions is their failure to offer any explanation for how al-Qaida could possibly be covered under the plain meaning of the text.

The Pentagon is revising the rules for interrogation. If we hope to succeed in the war on terror, the final product *must* allow interrogators to use stress techniques against unlawful combatants. Chris Mackey testifies to how "ineffective schoolhouse methods were in getting prisoners to talk." He warns that his team "failed to break prisoners who I have no doubt knew of terrorist plots or at least terrorist cells that may one day do us harm. Perhaps they would have talked if faced with harsher methods."

The stress techniques that the military has used to date are not torture; the advocates can only be posturing in calling them such. On its website, Human Rights Watch lists the effects of real torture: "from pain and swelling to broken bones, irreparable neurological damage, and chronic painful musculoskeletal problems...

[to] long-term depression, post-traumatic stress disorder, marked sleep disturbances and alterations in self-perceptions, not to mention feelings of powerlessness, of fear, guilt and shame." Though none of the techniques that Pentagon interrogators have employed against al-Qaida comes anywhere close to risking such effects, Human Rights Watch nevertheless follows up its list with an accusation of torture against the Bush administration.

The pressure on the Pentagon to outlaw stress techniques won't abate, as the American Civil Liberties Union continues to release formerly classified government documents obtained in a Freedom of Information Act lawsuit concerning detention and interrogation. As of late December, the memos have merely confirmed that the FBI opposes stress methods, though the press breathlessly portrays them as confirming "torture."

Human Rights Watch, the ICRC, Amnesty International, and the other self-professed guardians of humanitarianism need to come back to earth—to the real world in which torture means what the Nazis and the Japanese did in their concentration and POW camps in World War II; the world in which evil regimes, like those we fought in Afghanistan and Iraq, don't follow the Miranda rules or the Convention Against Torture but instead gas children, bury people alive, set wild animals on soccer players who lose, and hang adulterous women by truckloads before stadiums full of spectators; the world in which barbarous death cults behead female aid workers, bomb crowded railway stations, and fly planes filled with hundreds of innocent passengers into buildings filled with thousands of innocent and unsuspecting civilians. By definition, our terrorist enemies and their state supporters have declared themselves enemies of the civilized order and its humanitarian rules. In fighting them, we must of course hold ourselves to our own high moral standards without, however, succumbing to the utopian illusion that we can prevail while immaculately observing every precept of the Sermon on the Mount. It is the necessity of this fallen world that we must oppose evil with force; and we must use all the lawful means necessary to ensure that good, rather than evil, triumphs.

✿ REVIEW QUESTIONS

1. What is the torture narrative according to Mac-Donald? Why doesn't she accept it?
2. According to MacDonald, why didn't the Army's 16 interrogation approaches work on the Kandahar prisoners? How did the interrogators respond?
3. What nontraditional techniques were used on Mohamed al-Kahtani according to MacDonald?
4. How does MacDonald explain what happened at Abu Ghraib?

✿ DISCUSSION QUESTIONS

1. Do the stress techniques that MacDonald describes amount to torture or not? Should they be used for interrogation of prisoners? Explain your position.
2. Should interrogators be allowed to use water boarding, the most effective of the techniques? What is your view?

PROBLEM CASES

1. A Nuclear Bomb

Al Qaeda terrorists have planted a small nuclear device in an apartment building in London, and it is set to go off in two hours. If it goes off, it will kill thousands of people and injure thousands more. It will destroy a large part of the city. The terrorist group that planted the bomb has been under surveillance by the police. The police suspect that a devastating terrorist act has been planned; they have been monitoring telephone conversations and e-mails for months. They decide to bring in one of the terrorists for questioning. They know he has planned terrorist attacks in the past, and they have good evidence that a nuclear attack is going to happen in London and that he knows about it. The terrorist has been questioned before, and he knows the routine. If he refuses to talk, then the bomb will go off as he planned; his terrorist mission will be accomplished. Time is running out. There is not enough time to evacuate the city. The police are reasonably confident that the suspect knows where the bomb is and when it is set to go off. One of the policemen happens to have experience in torturing, although it is illegal and not normally used. The policeman believes the terrorist will talk if tortured.

Should the terrorist be tortured or not? If he does not talk, the bomb will go off as planned and thousands will die or be injured. But if he does reveal the location of the bomb, experts will rush to the location and they will be able to prevent it from detonating. Is torture justified in this situation? Why or why not?

2. The Extraordinary Rendition Program

(See Jane Mayer, "Outsourcing Torture," *The New Yorker,* February 14, 2005.) The extraordinary rendition program began as far back as 1995. Originally, it was directed at suspects having outstanding foreign arrest warrants, but after 9/11, the program was expanded to target suspected terrorists. Suspicious "enemy combatants" were captured and confined and interrogated in secret CIA prisons called "black sites" outside the United States. President Bush admitted the existence of prisons in a September 2006 speech. The most common destinations for suspects are Egypt, Jordan, Syria, and Morocco; all are known to practice torture and have been cited for human-rights violations by the State Department. An estimated 150 people have been rendered since 2001.

The legal status of the rendering program is controversial. In 1998, Congress passed legislation saying that the policy of the United States is not to expel, extradite, or otherwise affect the involuntary return of any person to a country where the person would be in danger of being subjected to torture. The American Civil Liberties Union claims that the United States is violating federal and international law by engaging in secret abductions and torture.

But Alberto Gonzales, the U.S. attorney general, argues that U.S. and international laws and prohibitions against torture do not apply to "enemy combatants" and do not apply to American interrogations of confined suspects overseas. On this view, suspected terrorists are basically outside the scope of the law. They can be detained indefinitely, without counsel, without charges of wrongdoing, and interrogated using CIA methods.

CIA sources have described six "Enhanced Interrogation Techniques" that are used to interrogate al Qaeda suspects confined in the secret prisons. The CIA interrogators are supposed to be trained and authorized to use these techniques:

1. Attention Grab: The interrogator forcefully grabs the shirt front of the prisoner and shakes him. Violent shaking can cause whiplash injuries.
2. Attention Slap: The prisoner is slapped in the face with the aim of causing pain and fear.
3. Belly Slap: The naked prisoner is slapped hard in the stomach to cause pain. A punch to the stomach can produce permanent internal damage.
4. Long Time Standing: This technique is very effective. Prisoners are forced to stand handcuffed with their feet shackled to an eyebolt in the floor for more than forty hours. They become exhausted and sleep deprived.
5. The Cold Cell: The naked prisoner is made to stand in a cell kept below fifty degrees and is regularly doused with cold water. The prisoner can die of hypothermia.
6. Water Boarding: The prisoner is bound to an inclined board with the feet raised and the head slightly below the feet. Cellophane is wrapped over the face. Water is poured on the face from a hose or a bucket. The gag reflex quickly kicks in with a terrifying fear of drowning. After a short time, the victim pleads for the treatment to stop.

Are these CIA methods torture or not? Suppose that these methods produce valuable information about al Qaeda terrorists and their future plans for attacks. If so, are these methods justified? What is your view? Should the United States continue the rendering program? Why or why not?

3. Khalid Sheik Mohammed

(See the Wikipedia article with links to news reports.) According to a transcript released by the military on March 15, 2007, Mr. Mohammed confessed to directing the 9/11 attacks and thirty-one other terrorist attacks and plans. He testified at the Guantanamo Bay detention facility that he was "responsible for the 9/11 attacks from A to Z." He described himself as al Qaeda's military operational commander for foreign operations. He claimed the he personally decapitated Daniel Pearl, the American journalist who was kidnapped and murdered in 2002 in Pakistan. He said he was responsible for several other operations, including the 2001 Richard Reid shoe bomber attempt to blow up an airliner, the 2002 Bali nightclub bombing in Indonesia, and the 1993 World Trade Center attack. He said he was involved in more than two dozen uncompleted terrorist plots, including ones that targeted offices in New York City, Los Angeles, and Chicago. He plotted to blow up nuclear power plants. He planned assassination attempts of several U.S. presidents. He planned to explode London's Big Ben tower and destroy the Panama Canal.

Mr. Mohammed was arrested in Pakistan in 2003 and "disappeared" to a semisecret prison in Jordan where he was interrogated by the CIA. His confession came after four years of captivity, including six months at Guantanamo Bay. CIA officials told ABC news that Mr. Mohammed's interrogation included water boarding. The technique involves strapping a prisoner on an inclined board with the head below the feet. The face is wrapped in cellophane and water poured over it. This produces an intense gag reflex and fear of drowning, but it is not supposed to result in permanent physical damage. The CIA officers who subjected themselves to the procedure lasted an average of fourteen seconds before giving up. Mr. Mohammed impressed the interrogators when he was able to last between two and two-and-a-half minutes before begging to confess.

The Human Rights Watch says that Mr. Mohammed was tortured. Do you agree? Should water boarding be acknowledged as torture? Why or why not?

The CIA officals admit that confessions resulting from torture or mistreatment may not be reliable. For example, Ibn al Shaykh al Libbi was water boarded and then made to stand naked in a cold cell overnight where he was regularly doused with cold water. After two weeks of "enhanced interrogation," his confessions became the basis for the Bush administration claim that Iraq trained al Qaeda members to use biochemical weapons. Later, it was established that he had no knowledge of such training or weapons and had fabricated the statements to avoid further harsh treatment.

Some commentators are skeptical about Mr. Mohammed's rambling and wide-ranging confessions. For example, Michigan Representative Mike Rogers, a Republican on the terrorism panel of the House Intelligence Committee, found the confessions to be exaggerated or self-promotional. He doubted that Mr. Mohammed had a role in so many terrorist acts and plans. One CIA official admitted that some of Mr. Mohammed's claims during interrogation were "white noise" designed to send the interrogators on "wild goose chases" or to "get him through the day's interrogation sessions."

If Mr. Mohammed's confessions were not useful or reliable, then was the CIA interrogation justified?

Suppose that the confessions in question produced useful information that prevented terrorist attacks. Would that fact justify the treatment Mr. Mohammed received at the hands of the CIA interrogators?

Now that he has confessed to crimes including murder, what should be done with Mr. Mohammed? The Bush administration position is that he is an "enemy combatant" without any legal rights. This means that he could be executed without a trial. Is this the right thing to do?

Another option is to hold him indefinitely at Guantanamo Bay or one of the secret CIA prisons. Is this a good idea?

Confessions or evidence based on torture are not admissible in U.S. civilian courts, but Mr. Mohammed could face a military trial or tribunal where his confessions are used as evidence against him. Would this be fair? What is your view?

4. *The Geneva Convention and the UN Convention*

The United States ratified the Geneva Convention relative to the Treatment of Prisoners of War in 1955. It prohibits "cruel treatment and torture." It also prohibits "outrages upon personal dignity, in particular, humiliating and degrading treatment."

The United Nations Convention Against Torture and Other Cruel, Inhuman or Degrading Treatment or Punishment was adopted by the UN General Assembly in 1984. To date, 142 nations have ratified it, including the United States.

Article 1 defines torture (in part) as "any act by which severe pain or suffering, whether physical or mental, is intentionally inflicted on a person for such purposes as obtaining from him or a third person information or a confession."

Article 2 requires each state to take "effective legislative, administrative, judicial or other measures to prevent acts of torture." It also says that no circumstances whatever, whether a state of war or a threat of war or any other public emergency, may be used to justify torture.

Article 3 prohibits a state from extraditing a person to another state to be tortured.

Article 16 states that each state that is a party to the agreement "shall undertake to prevent in any territory under its jurisdiction other acts of cruel, inhuman or degrading treatment or punishment which do not amount to torture as defined in Article 1."

Should the United States follow these conventions or not? Are violations of these conventions war crimes? What is your position?

✂ SUGGESTED READINGS

The Stanford Encyclopedia of Philosophy (http://plato.stanford.edu) has an excellent article on torture written by Seamus Miller. The CIA website (www.cia.gov) has detailed information on torture, including personal anecdotes, methods used, information gained, and so on. The World Organization Against Torture (www.omct.org) is a global network fighting against torture and other human rights violations.

Kenneth Roth and Minky Worden, eds., *Torture* (New York: New Press, 2005). This is a collection of twelve articles on torture, including Micahel Ignatieff on justifying torture, Jean Mendez on the victim's perspective, Jamie Feiner on torture in U.S. prisons, and David Rieff on the inadequacies of the human rights view.

Sanford Levison, ed., *Torture* (Oxford: Oxford University Press, 2006). This is a useful collection of seventeen essays covering the morality, legality, and practice of torture.

Fritz Allhoff, "Terrorism and Torture," *International Journal of Applied Philosophy* 17, 1 (2003): 105–118, supports the use of torture to get information about imminent and significant threats but not to force confession or to deter crime.

Fritz Allhoff, "A Defense of Torture," *International Journal of Applied Philosophy* 19, 2 (Fall 2005): 243–264, argues for the permissibility of torture in ticking-bomb cases.

Michael Davis, "The Moral Justification of Torture and Other Cruel, Inhuman, or Degrading Treatment," *International Journal of Applied Philosophy* 19, 2 (2005): 161–178, argues that the ticking-bomb case proves nothing because it relies on intuition, which is unreliable and fails to provide any justification.

Christopher W. Tindale, "Tragic Choices," *International Journal of Applied Philosophy* 19, 2 (Fall 2005): 209–222, defends an absolute prohibition of interrogational torture; he argues that the ticking-bomb scenarios are ill considered.

Larry May, "Torturing Detainees During Interrogation," *International Journal of Applied Philosophy* 19, 2 (Fall 2005): 193–208, argues that our humanity demands that suspected terrorists not be subject to torture when they are captured and imprisoned.

David Sussman, "What's Wrong with Torture?" *Philosophy and Public Affairs* 33 (December 2005): 1–33, defends the intuition that torture is a special type of wrong, and this explains why we find it more morally offensive than other ways of inflicting harm.

Seumas Miller, "Is Torture Ever Morally Justified?" *International Journal of Applied Philosophy* 19, 2 (2005): 179–192, argues that torture is morally justified in extreme emergencies, but it ought not to be legalized.

Jeremy Waldron, "Torture and Positive Law," *Columbia Law Review* 105, 6 (2005): 1681–1750, defends the legal prohibition of torture. This prohibition is not just one rule among others; it is a legal archetype that is emblematic of a basic commitment to nonbrutality in the legal system.

Alan M. Dershowitz, *Why Terrorism Works* (New Haven, CT: Yale University Press, 2002), devotes a chapter to defending the use of torture on terrorists to get information about imminent attacks.

Howard J. Curzer, "Admirable Immorality, Dirty Hands, Ticking Bombs, and Torturing Innocents," *Southern Journal of Philosophy* 44, 1 (Spring 2006): 31–56, argues that torturing is morally required and should be done when it is the only way to avert disasters. He admits that it is odd to hold that a vicious act like torture is morally required.

Jessica Wolfendale, "Training Torturers," *Social Theory and Practice* 322, 2 (April 2006): 269–287, argues that ticking-bomb arguments ignore the fact that permitting torture requires training torturers. This fact casts doubt on the arguments.

Karen J. Greenberg and Joshua L. Drafel, eds., *The Torture Papers* (Cambridge: Cambridge University Press, 2006), documents the abuse of prisoners at Abu Ghraib and Guantanamo.

Mark Danner, *Torture and Truth* (New York: New York Review of Books, 2004), argues that torture is part of a planned policy of the Bush administration.

Karen J. Greenberg, ed., *The Torture Debate in America* (Cambridge: Cambridge University Press, 2006), presents different perspectives on torture, from absolute prohibition to a useful weapon in the war on terrorism.

Colin Dayan, *The Story of Cruel and Unusual* (Boston: MIT Press, 2007), argues that recent Supreme Court decisions have dismantled the Eighth Amendment protection against "cruel and unusual" punishment. The result is the abuse and torture of prisoners at Abu Ghraib and Guantanamo.

William Sampson, *Confession of an Innocent Man* (Toronto: McClellan & Stewart, 2005). This is the horrifying story of an innocent Canadian man arrested, imprisoned, and tortured into confessing to car bombings he did not commit. Later, he was officially exonerated of the crimes.

Alfred McCoy, *A Question of Torture* (New York: Owl Books, 2006), describes the development of the torture methods used by the CIA.

Susan Sontag, "Regarding the Torture of Others," *The New York Times Magazine*, May 24, 2004, discusses the implications and meaning of the famous photographs of prisoners at Abu Ghraib.

INDEX